CW00349995

FISHING THROUGH THE APOCALYPSE

FISHING THROUGH THE APOCALYPSE

An Angler's Adventures in the 21st Century

MATTHEW L. MILLER

LYONS
PRESS

Guilford, Connecticut

An imprint of The Rowman & Littlefield Publishing Group, Inc.
4501 Forbes Blvd., Ste. 200
Lanham, MD 20706
www.rowman.com

Distributed by NATIONAL BOOK NETWORK

British Library Cataloguing in Publication Information available

Library of Congress Cataloging-in-Publication Data available

ISBN 978-1-4930-3741-4 (hardcover)
ISBN 978-1-4930-3742-1 (e-book)

♾™ The paper used in this publication meets the minimum requirements of American National Standard for Information Sciences—Permanence of Paper for Printed Library Materials, ANSI/NISO Z39.48-1992.

Printed in the United States of America

For Mom and Dad, Lana and Larry Miller

Once there were brook trout in the streams in the mountains . . . On their backs were vermiculate patterns that were maps of the world in its becoming. Maps and mazes. Of a thing which could not be put back. Not be made right again. In the deep glens where they lived all things were older than man and they hummed of mystery.

CORMAC MCCARTHY, *The Road*

The world seems so knackered. I just think a wild trout in London would mean that it wasn't.

CHARLES RANGELEY-WILSON, *City Fishing*

Contents

Acknowledgments

This book would not have been possible without the assistance of the many researchers, conservationists, fisheries managers, guides, and fellow anglers who lent me their expertise. They answered my questions, reviewed drafts, discussed big issues, and took me fishing. I cannot thank them enough for their generosity and patience.

My friend Solomon David deserves special "garcolades" as he has supported this project from the beginning, reviewed chapters, and championed my work within the fisheries research community.

While social media and online forums deservedly get a bad rap for keeping people out of the outdoors, I've found many online sources to be invaluable in researching this book, as well as a way to find hunting and fishing friends with similarly obscure interests. The folks at goodhunting.com were early supporters of my work. Roughfish.com provided inspiration, story ideas, and contacts for several chapters. The Twitter "fish nerd" community connected me to great researchers around the country.

Family friend Susie Campbell introduced me to people important to the Coal Creek chapter.

I've wanted to write about the outdoors since I was twelve years old. Many teachers, professors, and mentors encouraged that passion and kept me going when it seemed an impossible goal. In particular, I'm grateful to Bill Gallagher, Jim Ferguson, Frank Pisano, Jennifer Jackson, Gigi Marino, the late Jim Bashline, Michael Kincheloe, Rachel Larsen, and Bill Gafjken.

Ted Williams is a longtime writing hero who I'm now honored to call a colleague. Stephen Bodio was an early writing inspiration and is now a friend.

A shout out to the staff of Penn State's Center for the Performing Arts, the first place to employ me as a writer. I especially thank Robin Conklin, John Rafacz, and Renee Zeigler.

For the past seventeen years, I've been lucky enough to work for The Nature Conservancy with extraordinarily talented and gifted colleagues, too many to list here. Thanks to Bob Lalasz and Peter Kareiva for giving me a space to write creatively within the organization, at the *Cool Green Science* blog. My current supervisors, Hugh Possingham and Molly Wallace, have supported this project from the start, as have my science communications team members Cara Byington and Justine Hausheer. I have valued all the time and conversations with the Conservancy's excellent field staff, especially my friends Dayna Gross, Mike Eckley, Megan Grover-Cereda (and Trish Cereda), and my colleagues in the Boise office. And an extra special shout out to Laura Hubbard, supervisor extraordinaire, mentor, inspiration, and friend. I owe you more than can be repaid.

I am indebted to the members of the Outdoor Writers Association of America for your professional development advice and friendship over the years. I can't list you all, but I value all you have done for me. Kermit Henning introduced me to this organization when I was only twelve and has remained an enthusiastic supporter of my work. My talented colleague and friend Christine Peterson reviewed multiple chapters and provided excellent feedback. Brett Prettyman went above and beyond the call of duty, connecting me to sources for many chapters, as well as reviewing many of those chapters.

Thanks to the excellent fishing writer Stephen Sautner for advice and introductions in the early stages of this book, and to Eugene Brissie at Lyons Press for taking on this project. I appreciate the production staff of Lyons Press and Newgen for their copy editing, design, and expert advice, and for keeping this project on track.

I thank my in-laws, Dean and Connie Puffett, and the extended Puffett-Glass clan, for their support and for accommodating my unusual interests and road trips while in the Midwest. I am always buoyed by the energy and enthusiasm of my awesome nieces and nephews, Jacob, Jack, Samantha, David, Kelli, Tyler, Noah, Sarah, and Isaac.

My brother Mike has been a constant friend, source of laughs and Star Wars minutia, and is now my son's hero. My parents, Larry and Lana Miller, saw my love of the outdoors, books, and travel from an early age, and gave me every advantage so I could pursue those interests throughout my life. They provided a childhood that every nature-loving kid should have. Now, they enthusiastically read every word I write and are my biggest fans. The book is dedicated to them.

My son Derek reminds me that writing at the computer is best done in small doses, and that often it's time to quit wrestling words and instead dance, race cars, and chase each other around the house. Seeing everything anew from his eyes has been one of my life's greatest joys. I hope he can find his own passions that give his life meaning and purpose. Judging by his energy, that won't be a problem.

And Jennifer. Sometimes, words fail. You have been my greatest friend and partner in adventures near and far for more than twenty joyful years. Your sense of humor, your love, and your enthusiasm keep me grounded. You not only accept my absences during my often-strange outdoor adventures, you deal with the pestilence I bring home, a list that includes shingles, fungal infections, severe poison ivy, septic wounds, various bites, all manner of horrible odors, and, most recently, bedbugs. And yet, you have done nothing but buoy my spirits during this book. You read and reviewed every page. You're my constant. I couldn't have done it without you.

INTRODUCTION:
FISHING THROUGH THE APOCALYPSE

I watched my worm sink slowly into the murk: past a floating beer bottle, past a submerged tire, finally disappearing into a jagged hole in a rusty filing cabinet. I wondered if this spot could hold fish. Or any life, really.

Large, overstuffed garbage bags lined the bottom of the drainage ditch. The water pooled up between the road and a large farm field, although "farm field" probably conjures the wrong image. The scene more resembled a factory, with workers and machines bustling: spraying, pruning, harvesting.

The rumbling of a truck broke my concentration. Overloaded with fruit, it barreled by me, inches from my back. I caught my breath and balance, but seconds later a jacked-up hot rod, rap music blaring, careened in my direction. I tried to make eye contact with the driver, but he was texting. I briefly contemplated jumping into the rancid, watery ditch just as the driver glanced up and veered into the center of the road.

I was risking my life for one of the world's nastiest fishing holes.

It seemed a fitting end to the day. I had planned the weekend as a fishing tour of urban and agricultural canals across South Florida, searching for various fish oddities. I knew Florida's canals teemed with an array of introduced species—many of them from tropical environs—and I planned to catch as many as I could. I figured the possibility of catching snakehead and walking catfish and colorful cichlids would compensate for any obstacle I encountered.

I figured wrong.

⌒

The day I fished the trash hole began with such promise. I awoke in the predawn humidity in a cabin in the Everglades, still aglow from my previous day's fishing. I had cast my flies to large snook and aggressive ladyfish in national park backcountry. It was one of those days that is celebrated in sporting magazines. I saw manatees and sawfish, showy spoonbills and squawking herons. The fishing proved tough but not impossible. Snook darted out of mangrove roots to hammer streamers.

Those memories still buzzing in my head, I motored out of the Everglades into the urban reality just to the east. I gulped hot coffee and snarfed a pack of Pop-Tarts to a nostalgic soundtrack of eighties' pop tunes. Whatever came my way, I was ready.

The first stop immediately gave me pause. A friend sent me directions to a little canal just off the interstate, claiming it the best spot to find brown hoplo catfish, a cool-looking, armored Asian species now swimming in South Florida waters. I stepped out of the car to an overpowering stench, an assault of stale urine and rotting food.

The coffee turned in my stomach. I stepped over a discarded condom into the grassy strip bordering the canal and felt my water sandal squish into something slimy. I lifted my sandal to see it covered in brown, fecal goo. For the first time in my life, I hoped—nay, prayed—I had just stepped in dog shit. Given the surroundings, the discarded toilet paper, and the odor, I recognized this as wildly wishful thinking.

I peered into the water and immediately saw a large brown hoplo catfish finning below me. I returned to the car and dutifully retrieved my rod and tackle. The fish didn't bite. I hardly noticed.

I spent my time watching my step in what turned out to be one big open-air toilet.

Regret creeped in. I had a free day in South Florida. I could be casting flies in the Everglades. I could be dodging alligators instead of piles of excrement. I could be standing with a field guide and binoculars ticking birds off my life list. But I wanted to experience urban canal fishing, and catch wild new species, and so I pressed on. The rest of the day didn't improve. I failed to see fish but saw plenty of floating junk. I felt ridiculous as I cast lines in strip mall ditches. At one pull-off, a retiree on a road trip from Canada strolled over. "There actually fish in this?" he asked.

"That's what I'm trying to find out," I replied.

"This where you locals fish?"

"I'm not a local. I'm from Idaho."

He backed way, walking briskly back to his waiting spouse, apparently eager to tell her about the nut job he just found. I can't say I blamed him.

I continued along my planned route, although the novelty of urban fishing had long since worn off. And that brought me to the spot with the rusty filing cabinet. An online acquaintance had called it "a gem, a secret little spot with all kinds of weird fish." This was a guy who described himself as a "life lister"—he traveled the world seeking new species of fish.

Try as I might, I couldn't turn this spot into a "gem." What I saw was a slimy pool of water that doubled as the local garbage heap, requiring an angler to perch precariously along a road used in equal measure by local motorheads and large agribusiness shippers.

As I stood between toxic water and deadly road, the tip of my rod bounced, so subtly that at first I wondered if I imagined it. I pulled up and the little ultralight bent. A fish.

I reeled my line up, horsing the fish out of the discarded filing cabinet. The fish jerked as I gently lifted it out of the water. The hand-sized fish was a dark grayish hue, with a large black spot on each side. Its top fin extended beyond the body.

I identified it as a black acara, a species native to the Orinoco and Amazon basins of South America. At some point, a Floridian likely had seen some black acaras in a pet shop and thought they'd make cool pets. But the fish grew, and bashed against the aquarium's glass, and needed to be fed, so the owner unceremoniously dumped them in a ditch. The black acaras found the conditions of South Florida not so unlike the Amazon, and they bred and prospered.

Like the tires, the used condoms, and the discarded office equipment, the fish I held in my hand was another piece of junk in the ditch. Someone had bought it, used it, then threw it away. But in the case of the black acara, it swam on. Survived.

I released it back into its dystopian pond, and it immediately darted back into the refuge of the cabinet.

I set off on this journey to see what the future held for freshwater fish and the people who pursued them. But are toxic ditches filled with exotic fish really the end game? Will someday anglers be forced to sneak around the margins of an overcrowded hell, dangling worms into a trash heap?

⚬

Like many youth in rural America, I began fishing farm ponds at a young age with my dad and grandfathers. We'd use worms we just dug by the chicken coop, then cast them to bluegills and largemouth bass, sometimes keeping fish for dinner.

Fishing was just one component of a life outdoors. I was perhaps the poster child for what Edward O. Wilson calls biophilia, the inborn attraction to living creatures. I read about them and watched the wildlife documentaries on TV, but I also wanted to be out there among them. I hunted deer and squirrels, followed tracks in the snow, pored over field guides of birds and reptiles, captured insects, called owls, and walked through the woods just to see what I could see.

When I was fourteen, my dad took me along on a buddies fishing trip to Canada. I imagine my dad's friends worried I'd be a nuisance. They spent much of the time in the cabin eating steaks and drinking beer, talking about jobs and marriages. I fished. I fished when the sun came up and stayed out long after it had set, catching perch and crappies and rock bass, even the occasional pike. I fell asleep with the calls of loons echoing in my ears. I didn't want to leave. I wanted my life to be a fishing trip.

By college, my fishing focus shifted to bass fishing, casting minnows to largemouth bass in a nearby lake, and casting spinners and plugs to smallmouths. When I took a job with my alma mater, Penn State, I had more time to explore the streams, and turned to fly fishing for trout, an interest that continued when I moved to Idaho with its blue-ribbon spring creeks and mountain freestone rivers.

I'm not alone in this interest. The American Sportfishing Association estimates that more than forty-five million people go fishing in the United States in any given year. Around the world, millions of people fish for sport, for subsistence, and for a living. If there's water, there's a good chance there's someone trying to fish in it.

People even go fishing when they're paid *not* to fish. Behavioral economist Sheila Walsh Reddy tells of her work on Kiribati, a chain of islands in the Pacific that relies primarily on fish and coconuts for income. As the population grew, the local fishery showed signs of overharvest. Big fish numbers declined. The government began a social welfare program that increased payments for coconuts by 30 percent. By paying people more for coconuts, the reasoning went, people would fish less.

Instead, they fished *more*. As Reddy writes, "The men and women we talked to were earning more money in less time. This meant that they had extra time. And, what did they want to do with that time? Go fishing. The explanation hit me like the bumper sticker you see: 'A bad day of fishing beats a good day of working.'"

If you've ever cast a dry fly to a rising trout, or spent an afternoon pulling in bluegills with your kids, you probably understand. Fishing is fun. Catching fish is fun. It's a way to connect to nature.

A way to spend time outdoors with family and friends. We relive memories of past fish won and lost, and dream of trips to nearby lakes and faraway destinations.

Standing by an alpine lake does indeed feel better than sitting in front of an office computer. This is real life, we tell ourselves. The real world. What it's supposed to be like. Wild and untrammeled. I know. I live for that feeling.

Except this: Oftentimes, looks are deceiving. Much of the fishing we experience in the 21st century is in reality no less unnatural than pulling Amazonian fish from a trash-strewn Miami canal. The aesthetics may be more pleasing, but the situation is just as synthetic. We just can't see it through the haze of nostalgia and the pleasure of a fish on a line.

There's an important part of my youthful fishing that I ignored for many years. Four generations of my family owned land along a good-sized stream, and none of us ever fished it. Not once. And for good reason: It had no fish, or any other life, for that matter.

It's perhaps my true home water, more so than the farm ponds where I reeled in sunfish or the little creeks where I netted minnows and crayfish. This creek ran orange with the acid from mine drainage. It smelled of sulfur and a faint whiff of sewage. Coal dust and the remnants of mining lined the banks. That acid mine drainage rendered it a dead river.

As odd as it seems now, as a kid it was perfectly normal. I'd walk along and shoot my .22 rifle at the cans and bottles lining the banks, the *rat-tat-tat* of the shots echoing off coal heaps. A flowing, beautiful river? Please. More like a wasteland, a watery dump.

Recently, I read John Waldman's telling book, *Running Silver: Restoring Atlantic Rivers and Their Great Fish Migrations*. The author drew on extensive research to portray Eastern US rivers of yore: rivers running with millions of shad, eels, and more. Abundance. The book illustrates a phenomenon ecologists call "shifting baseline syndrome." Basically: what you grow up with, you consider normal. If that's an orange, smelly, dead stream, then that is the stream you accept. If you envision a river filled with migratory fish, your mind goes to Alaska. Not this reeking mess in front of you.

Or, as my fish conservationist colleague Mark Davidson is fond of saying, "You lose the memory, you lose the fish."

Once those fish are gone, it's very, very hard to get them back.

As an angler, many of the waters I fish have been impoverished in similar ways. A history of abuse has irrevocably damaged so many streams, rivers, and lakes. Invasive species, mismanagement, dams, pollution, climate change, and other threats have taken a heavy toll on freshwater habitats across the country.

And anglers have not always helped. Yes, fishing enthusiasts love to point to what they've contributed to conservation, but there's another side of the story. They've transported popular game species around the globe, decimating native species in the process. They've persecuted native species they've viewed as competitors or "trash" fish. Some anglers even push for genetically engineered fish that are more colorful or easier to catch.

With a growing human population and ever-increasing threats to freshwater habitats, I do not want to lose the memory of what it means to fish now, in this place. I know that, in some places, fishing has become downright weird: ponds that offer (for a fee) unlimited endangered species, fishing guides that use drones to catch "river monsters," or agencies that stock hatchery-produced mutants to attract angler interest.

I write about conservation for a living, and when you spend every day interviewing experts about the state of the world, you become acutely aware of Aldo Leopold's warning that "to have an ecological conscience is to live in a world of wounds."

But doom and gloom isn't motivating, and it's also not even remotely the whole story. Anglers also have led the charge in restoring native fish, in righting past wrongs. There are fisheries biologists, managers, guides, and sport fishers who are working to better manage our most popular species, to appreciate the unappreciated fish, to clean our waters, and protect public lands.

As an angler and conservationist, I sought to remove my preconceived notions about what it means to fish in the 21st century. I wanted to see what fishing was like, right now, in all its warts and glory.

I brought my naturalist's curiosity and my desire to catch any fish I encountered, large or small, native or alien. I did not want to inventory all the environmental wrongs facing rivers and lakes across the continent. Rather, I wanted to head out and explore the 21st century, fishing rod in hand.

On my journey, I'd encounter some of the most popular sport fishes, but I'd see them in a whole new light. I also confess to having a love of the more obscure species. On the edges, I found, is where you can see the promises and perils of freshwater fishing in America.

In this country, we still have remarkable fishing, and fish, as well as conservation successes that have restored things close to like they were in the "old days." Fishing can help us continue on that hopeful path to the future, but we're going to have to pay attention.

∼

Back in South Florida, I wondered if casting in a garbage-filled hole could tell me much of anything. I wondered if I had wandered a step too far. Still, I cast again into the little pool, my worm floating to rest on a bag of garbage. I heard a loud engine revving. I had already caught a fish here. This was not fishing's future. It felt like a stunt. I had been fishing in enough places to know that better options still exist.

I threw my rod in the car, and took off, eager to leave this spot. I drove round the bend, and saw four Latino men standing along the road. They still wore overalls caked in grime: they clearly had just walked from the adjacent industrial agricultural field.

They were fishing: three had beat-up spinning rods and one had a long, fiberglass pole with line tied on at the end. As I slowed down, I could see them laughing and gesturing to each other, just a group of friends enjoying a bit of recreation during their time off.

As I looked, I realized they were fishing a ditch that connected to the cesspool I had just departed. For them, this was not a stunt. Blue-ribbon trout streams and even Everglades mangroves were far out of reach, a fantasy. This was their present, their reality: fishing that involved casting lines into polluted, junk-filled holes surrounded by agricultural monoculture and a megacity.

They were fishing through the apocalypse.

— Matthew L. Miller
Boise, Idaho, June 2018

CHAPTER ONE

Banana-Rama

I stepped out of the car and gagged, so overpowering was the stench of dead fish and rot. I had come to expect foul smells during my travels to questionable canals and urban ponds, but this odor brought tears to my eyes. I knew this region of rural Idaho contained many confined dairy operations, which packed their own potent smells, but the scent of bad fish easily overpowered any trace of manure.

My wife, Jennifer, had work to do nearby, and she looked at me uncertainly. "You're really going to fish here?" she asked.

I nodded. Jennifer is no stranger to my peculiar ideas of fun. She has spent days of an overseas vacation searching for aardvarks, and she has grown used to me stalking canals and urban ponds with a fishing rod. But this wasn't quirky. It just stank.

"I'm not fishing right here," I said. "I'll hike in to other ponds."

"It smells," she replied. "And I won't be able to pick you up until this afternoon."

I assured her I'd be fine, gathered up my gear, and headed out. Within a few steps, the stench only worsened, and I immediately regretted my decision. I swiveled back toward the car, but Jennifer had already pulled out. I looked at my cell phone: no signal.

Before me two drained ponds revealed the source of the stench: hundreds of dead fish baked in the sun. A sign informed me that these two fishing ponds had been drained because invasive carp had overtaken them. The only effective way to control the carp, it stated, was to kill all the fish and start from scratch. Personnel would refill the water and restock with game fish soon.

I looked, briefly, at the carp carcasses, many bloated into grotesque footballs in the 80-degree heat. I might have been sympathetic to the management regime, but for the reason for the day's trip: I was here to catch genetic mutants. These mutants were considerably less natural than the carp; they existed solely because of human breeding and factory farm production. But, unlike the carp, they weren't being controlled. In fact, a fresh batch was stocked here every few weeks.

Fortunately, a series of other small "lakes" remained undrained and well stocked with trout a short walk away. I continued on, eager to put the sickly odor of death behind me. The scenery improved, but barely. My path took me by concrete run after concrete run: the Hagerman Fish Hatchery, an Idaho Department of Fish and Game facility where hundreds of thousands of trout are produced, including the ones I was about to attempt to catch. I had the admittedly ridiculous thought that I should just cast into the hatchery runway. Unsporting? Well, transport these same trout 200 yards and dump them in a pond, and anglers would line up for them.

I walked that short distance, and, sure enough, about twenty anglers stood and sat (mostly sat) around the pond, watching bobbers. I appeared to be the only one bearing a fly rod. I found an empty stretch of bank and began scanning for my quarry. I saw a few silvery shadows dart by but didn't even attempt to cast. I'd know my quarry when I saw it. And I had no doubt I would see it, as these fish were created so that anglers wouldn't have to look too hard.

I didn't wait long. Like a swimming neon sign, the shimmering form drifted my way. While many called its color "golden," this was not the gold of a goldfish, but more the bright yellow of a marshmallow Easter chick. I cast my beadhead pheasant tail nymph, a fly that seemed oddly inappropriate for the occasion and location. I wished for a glob of glittery PowerBait.

The fly landed. The fish gave it a look but continued swimming. Ten minutes later, another neon fish—exotic yet inarguably a trout—swam by. I cast about 10 feet ahead of it, my nymph sinking but held up by a foam indicator—my own version of bobber fishing.

This time, the trout darted toward the fly and inhaled it. I lifted the three-weight fly rod, and it made an initial frantic run. Maybe due to the heat or maybe due to its general frailty, it gave up the fight rather quickly. After a couple of darts, it barely wiggled. I pulled it into the net and stared at the fish before me.

Some called this fish a palomino trout or golden rainbow. Douglas M. Thompson, in his environmental history of trout fishing, called it a "what-the-hell-is-that trout." I preferred a local nickname: banana trout.

In hand, the neon color seemed to fade, and it resembled the dirty pale of an over-used white dishrag. I stared at this strange creature. It seemed fake, and I felt the same sensation as watching a computer-generated dinosaur. No matter how real they make it, you can't shake the idea that it's an inferior copy of something magnificent. Still, the fish I held in my hand represented so much of the history of trout fishing in America. And if we aren't careful, it could be the symbol of the future.

In 1955, a West Virginia state fish hatchery worker noticed, sticking out among the dense schools of rainbows in the concrete runway, a yellow-hued trout swimming around. This wasn't an albino but rather a trout exhibiting a rare genetic mutation. In the wild, such a fish would quickly become easy prey for a heron or a mink. Its odds of reaching adulthood are likely lower than you winning the lottery without buying a ticket.

In the hatchery, on the other hand, this fish was recognized as a—if you'll pardon the pun—golden opportunity. The employee extracted the fish from its fellow hatchery mates, and reared it in isolation. He gave the fish an ironic nickname, Little Camouflage, and launched a program to select for this mutation. Within eight years, careful breeding had produced enough yellow trout for West Virginia to stock for recreational fishing. They were rather grandiosely named Centennial golden trout, and became an instant hit—a source of such pride that this trout is now the symbol of the state's fisheries program.

Other states soon got in the act, with both agency hatcheries and fishing clubs stocking these neon fish as novelties. Much of the history of American angling has consisted of the fishing community trying to make all waters contain the same species. Apparently, even for those who only want rainbow trout, catching the same thing over and over can get old. Having a bright, new fish adds some excitement to the visit to the local "put-and-take" stream.

I caught my banana trout in Idaho, where the stocking program for these mutants is fairly modest. Hagerman, Idaho, sits near an area known as Thousand Springs, named for the gushing, clear water that dumps out of the Snake River Canyon's walls. Those springs originate in the mountains of Central Idaho, where they flow as typical Rocky Mountain rivers. But as the rivers descend into the sagebrush desert, they run through the area of Craters of the Moon National Monument, an extensive lava field. The water sinks into the porous lava but continues flowing, deep underground.

Other rivers and creeks east of the monument infiltrate into the groundwater, helping create one of the country's largest aquifer systems. The water flows 100 miles underground before bursting out of the Snake River's canyon walls. The journey takes some two hundred years; the water emerges crystal clear and purified. The springs are still there, but now Dozen Springs might be more accurate. Much of the water has been reappropriated for power, for intensive agriculture, and for aquaculture. Certainly, the acres of fish farms hold some surprises. One operator raises sturgeon as a sustainable substitute for Russian caviar. Some produce another food fish, tilapia (and these fish are occasionally caught in the adjacent Snake River, proof of the difficulty in containing hatchery fish). Local restaurants even serve locally grown fried alligator, which also fuels the inevitable rumors about free-ranging reptiles in the river.

Mainly, the hatcheries produce trout—more trout than anywhere else in the country. Most of these fish are destined for human consumption. When you order a trout fillet at your favorite restaurant, there's a good chance it once swam within a few miles of where I fished for banana trout.

State and federal hatcheries also tap the cold water for fish production, both to raise endangered species and to stock fish for people to catch. With the widespread availability of trout, there's room for a little novelty. A private aquaculture facility supplies about twenty thousand banana trout to the state hatchery. A lot of those trout don't survive to reach stocking age, but there's still enough to release a few thousand for anglers each year. Most of these are destined for the wildlife management area ponds adjacent to the hatchery's concrete runs.

"Most people like them," says Joe Chapman, the Hagerman hatchery's manager. "There are purists who don't because they're unnatural. There are people who think they're just a goldfish or a carp. But most people like the novelty."

Chapman says Idaho followed neighboring Utah's lead. He relates an oft-told story about Utah's trout stocking program: Fishermen believed the Utah Department of Wildlife weren't stocking as many trout as was claimed. To counter these claims, agency officials added banana trout to the mix. "Anglers could see them, so even if they weren't catching fish, they knew trout were there," Chapman says.

He believes these trout have a lot to recommend them for stocking. "They grow fast, and they seem to deal with rising water temperatures better," he says.

Many local anglers claim that they're also harder to catch, and Chapman says there may be some truth to that. "Right after we stock them, they're dumb as rocks and easy to catch. That's true for all hatchery fish," he says. "After they see their siblings get yanked out, they smarten up really quick. And I think the goldens get even more finicky. They can be a real challenge."

In fact, when I talked to him after my outing, he said that the banana trout see so many worms and globs of PowerBait that they quickly wise up to them. Small, golden spoons, spinners and flies work much better. So my nymph wasn't such a bad choice after all.

Despite their purported wariness, many serious anglers spurn them. As an adult, it's hard to take banana trout seriously. You won't see one of these yellow beauties on the cover of an outdoor magazine, and woe to the Facebook poster who puts up a banana trout hero shot on a Facebook fishing forum. Douglas Thompson, in *The Quest for the Golden Trout*, writes, "It was clear to me that this fish is a symbol for much of what is wrong with coldwater fish management."

Perhaps the banana trout destroys any illusion of wildness. You can catch a hatchery rainbow and perhaps lie to yourself that it is actually a wild fish. You can't do that with a banana trout. You know it was only recently swimming around a concrete run, gulping pellets. For this reason, perhaps all stocked fish should be bananas. Then maybe anglers could acknowledge the reality, the reality that much of 21st-century fishing relies on similarly unnatural fish.

In the late 1800s, many rivers and streams were overfished, and some feared interest in angling was waning. Americans looked around and didn't like what they saw: the frontier vanishing, taking wildlife and outdoor living with it. From this loss, the American conservation movement launched, including many of this country's greatest ideas like national parks and wetlands protection. Early conservationists believed that to protect and restore fish, managers had to raise them and stock them in streams so that anglers would have a perpetual supply.

Rainbow trout are native to many rivers and waters that are or were connected to the Pacific Ocean. They also proved to be a hardy fish that could easily be propagated in captivity. In 1875, rainbow trout eggs were sent to New York from California. The propagation and stocking of non-native game fish has been a major aspect of fishing and fisheries management ever since. It essentially defines the story of sport fishing in the 20th century.

Freshwater fish face many well-documented problems, of course, including big ones like climate change, dams, and loss of water. But as I traveled, again and again, it struck me just how often the biggest challenge facing native fish species was invasive species. That's no surprise for any conservationist, or even angler. But when we think about aquatic invasives, we think about zebra mussels or those carp that dominated the wildlife management area's pond. Our mind goes to obvious villains, like the snakehead lurking in the Potomac. A more uncomfortable truth is this: Many of the worst invasives are game fish, stocked in waters on purpose, by and on behalf of sport fishers. Even in seemingly pristine national parks and wilderness, you will find non-native game fish, put there on purpose.

Take rainbow trout. The fish's acolytes stocked them far beyond their native range in the West, and even beyond the United States—a history told brilliantly in Anders Halverson's *An Entirely Synthetic Fish*. Famous trout fisheries in New Zealand and Patagonia are built entirely with non-native trout. You can fish for rainbow trout in the Himalayas and in the small African country of Lesotho.

Fisheries managers boast of their scientific approach, but this science belongs to modern livestock production, not wildlife biology. As that science progressed, other fish species soon joined rainbow trout on the hatchery list: brown and brook trout, smallmouth and largemouth bass, bluegill, walleye, and striped bass. Some provided fisheries in the new habitats created by reservoirs and in the tailwaters below reservoir discharges. Managers also dumped a shocking number of fish into streams and rivers with enthusiasm and ambition, but apparently without any reflection on the havoc they were about to wreak on stream ecology.

"Many trout were shipped out west in trains," says Helen Neville, senior scientist for Trout Unlimited. "When the train would stop, people would dump the fish in any nearby stream."

Adventurous conservationists even hitched buckets filled with non-native trout on mules and packed them deep in the wilderness. This stocking fervor created new fisheries—fish were stocked in alpine lakes devoid of fish, for instance.

The stocking also created some strange scenarios. Brook trout (actually a char) have struggled in many of their native streams of the Eastern United States, as they need clean, cold water. They've been slammed with habitat degradation, acid rain, water pollution, and, yes, introduction of exotic species like brown trout from Europe. But in the West, where they were stocked by the bucket load, brook trout have thrived, completely dominating many waters. Even the most fervent trout stocking defenders draw the line at Western brook trout, as the fish proliferate to a degree that the stream is filled with stunted fish.

Even rainbow trout themselves have suffered, at least the native varieties. The initial trout for the hatchery program were captured in California's McCloud River. But very early on, perhaps with that first shipment of eggs, unique trout subspecies and strains were mixed together. In the Rockies, you'll see a history of geological upheaval written in the rocks, in canyons and buttes and lava fields and jagged peaks. That upheaval created lengthy river systems, isolated streams and lakes that were periodically connected and disconnected to the flowing waters. The original rainbow trout form, known as steelhead, migrated from ocean to river like salmon. But the isolated rainbows adapted to different freshwater environments. Some found themselves in lakes filled with invertebrates and bulked up to tremendous sizes. Some lived in hot desert streams and survived temperatures that would turn other trout belly up in minutes. And many exhibited vibrant palettes of color on their sides, among the most beautiful of fish.

The hatchery system mixed these varieties into what author Anders Halverson calls in *An Entirely Synthetic Fish* "a single new mongrel species." These hatchery fish were dull silvery imitations of their wild cousins. Even worse, they were dumped by the truckload in streams with genetically pure and unique native subspecies—reducing so much diversity into a depressing monoculture.

This is undoubtedly bad for fish, but it's also bad for fishermen. Many anglers pat themselves on the back about their knowledge of nature, proud that they know waters in a way a mere spectator never could. And yet, many of the waters they fish are filled with exotic mongrels, and they don't care.

As Halverson said in an interview with Colorado University: "There's a fascinating paradox about fishing. A lot of anglers see fishing as an escape of civilization and industrialization or a spiritual escape from society. Yet you have a paradox that most of the fish they catch are the product of industrialization."

Indeed, the stocking continues at an industrial pace. In some waters, you can easily give in to the illusion that it's not even happening. My local trout water, the Boise River, has a self-reproducing population of rainbows, but thousands of fish are also stocked there each year. I can wade down to the river and almost convince myself that the nice rainbow on my line is a wild fish, but I can't really know.

In many situations, there's not even an illusion. The annual sportsman's show at the county fairgrounds has a large inflatable pool filled with trout. Kids can stand around it and "fish" for those trout. You never see an adult do this, of course. You couldn't dangle a line into a swimming pool and not feel a fool. And yet, many ponds, streams and reservoirs offer *exactly* the same fishing situation, just in a more "natural" setting.

When I lived in Central Pennsylvania, I used to fish a small lake near my apartment every week. The fishing here was for bass, stocked when the lake was originally dammed but otherwise wild. I knew that every April, trout were stocked in the dam's spillway for the opening of Pennsylvania's trout season. Since I had caught about every other species from this property, I figured I'd add rainbow trout to the list.

When I arrived at 6:30 a.m., the parking lot resembled a Penn State football game, albeit one with a lot more pickup trucks and camouflage. Anglers lined the banks elbow to elbow at the pool below the spillway. Many, but not all, accompanied kids. I looked for a place to stand, and one fellow moved over and indicated I could join him. Kids began whining, impatient for the official 7:00 a.m. start. At 6:55, a youngster could stand it no more and let loose with a cast.

A gruff old man yelled "Close enough!" and immediately the air filled with a spiderweb of fishing line, bobbers and hooks festooned with worms, corn, marshmallows, and glittery PowerBait. Despite the inevitable tangles, it took seconds before the assembled crowd began pulling in trout after trout—all dumped there the day before. I cast out and immediately had a fish on.

Within forty-five minutes, I had a limit of fish as had nearly everyone else. Some of the bigger groups kept fishing but it was clear that most of the fish were gone. And so ended the trout fishing for the year. I returned to this spillway a few months later with a fly rod. I caught bluegills, largemouth bass, black crappie, and fallfish, but there wasn't a hint of trout. The water was too warm. The trout were placed just prior to the April 15 opener, but very few would live to see April 16. In the parlance of fisheries management, it was a "put-and-take" fishery. They put the fish in, and anglers are expected to take them out.

Farther from home, I visited the White River of Arkansas, a large tailwater and one of the most fabled trout fishing rivers in the Southern United States. Of course, trout historically did not swim in the White, but the cold waters below the dam created perfect habitat—another subplot of the trout story in America. While most serious fly fishers scorn opening day shenanigans, they travel far and pay big money to fish tailwaters.

My first day, I cast all morning and hadn't had a bite. A man in overalls walked by carrying a stringer full of trout.

"What are they hitting on?" I asked hopefully.

"It's not what, it's where," said the man. "See those PVC tubes going down to the river?"

I had seen them spaced along the river canyon. They ran from the parking lot down into the water.

"That's how they stock the trout," the man continued. "They don't want to walk them down to the water, so they just put the trout from the truck into those tubes and they slide right into the river. So the key is to fish right by those tubes. It's best right after they stock, but a lot of the fish stick right around there."

So, yes, I fished in public waters on a famous river, but was this really any different than dunking a worm in a fairground tub? Later, I walked farther upriver and caught a cutthroat trout—a fish eliminated from much of its western range by rainbow trout, but a non-native species here. A most befitting catch. A few casts later I caught an Ozark sculpin, a fat, bizarre fish that appeared as if it was all head. Most anglers considered it bait for trophy brown trout. I considered it the most interesting thing I had caught all day, one small sign of native species still here.

⌐∾⌐

The banana trout, by current standards, seems like watching an episode of the old cartoon *The Jetsons*. It's a vision of the future that now seems worn and dated, even quaint. Selective breeding and genetic engineering have come a long way. If a cloned super trout seems far-fetched, you're not paying attention. Never mind that the technology is there: one of the first wild animal species to be cloned was the white-tailed deer, an effort funded by the Texas hunting industry. Fisheries managers and the fishing industry also seek to produce fish that are bigger, stronger, meaner.

Ted Williams, one of the harshest critics of hatchery mutant fish (and one of the staunchest defenders of native species), writes of immense, grotesque rainbow trout that have shattered world records. Triploid syndrome, an extremely rare chromosomal abnormality (in the wild), occurs when an individual has three sets of chromosomes instead of the normal two. But commercial trout farms are creating triploid trout on purpose.

Williams explains,

> *Triploids are created by shocking fertilized eggs with heat, pressure or chemicals (doubtless in bell towers with the assistance of cackling hunchbacks). The third chromosome makes females sterile and males nearly so. Energy that would normally go to gonads is diverted to growth. So triploids frequently attain immense and unnatural size, acquire pinheads, diminutive tails and Jabba the Hutt physiques.*

Most of these fish are produced for the aquaculture industry, where, as with any livestock production, the producers value fast-growing animals. Some escape, which end up as recognized but dubious world records. And as even Williams admits, planting sterile triploid trout reduces the invasive threat posed by so many stockings.

But where does it end? Hybridization, crossing two species, has long been common and accepted in state fisheries programs, including such common ones as "tiger trout" (a brook crossed with brown trout), "wiper" (striped and white bass), and splake (lake and brook trout). Privately funded efforts to produce "super bass"—often with the intent of breaking the world record, are celebrated in mainstream outdoor magazines.

It's not hard to envision a future where every trout in a stream surpasses the 20th-century world record. Perhaps they'll dazzle with day-glo colors that put the poor banana trout to shame. Anglers could cast to extinct species bred to attack every lure with fervor.

But can we still delude ourselves that our hooks and lines connect us to the natural world? Can we even make that claim now, given our world of hatchery mongrels and mutants?

Environmental historian Douglas Thompson ends his scholarly look at trout fishing in *The Quest for the Golden Trout* by informing the reader that his fly rod is gathering dust. He urges readers to take off their rose-colored glasses and see fishing for what it is. He suggests that perhaps fishing is entirely an illusion. But perhaps he's not looking hard enough.

Because even in the heart of the country's commercial trout farming region, there's a better way. Months after my encounter with the banana trout, I parked in a dirt road pull-off up a rocky canyon just 10 miles away from the pale trout and bloated carp of the hatchery grounds. Marmots chirped from the ledges as a golden eagle passed overhead. I walked up along the Caribbean-blue stream before me. While many of the "Thousand Springs" have disappeared from the Hagerman Valley, and it's hard to imagine wildness amidst the factory farms and irrigated fields, it's still here. The wild heart of the region still beats, if you're willing to look.

I cast my fly and immediately a little trout smacked it. I lifted the rod and felt its thrashing. I pulled in a 6-inch fish, about as big as they ever get here. It was dark, almost black, with a bright orange tip on its dorsal fin. Was that gold tip a sign of another hatchery mutant? I waded through files, and found studies that determined these trout were natives, a unique strain found in this creek. Waterfalls and dams kept them isolated from the main river, which in this case kept them somewhat safe from the hatchery stockings and aquaculture escapees.

Whenever I've been fortunate to encounter wild rainbow trout, I'm struck with their beauty, the vibrant colors and spotting patterns. I marvel at how adapted the fish are to their respective streams. In this case, the blackish coloration must provide ideal camouflage among the dark lava rocks lining the stream bed. The perfect opposite of a banana trout.

Nearly every cast resulted in a strike. None of the fish I landed was larger than 6 inches. None was especially wary. You might argue that it's more of a challenge to catch a banana trout. Still, for reasons that may be inexplicable, I return to this stream any chance I get. I've never felt the urge for more of the banana-rama.

When you see the anglers sitting around a freshly stocked pond, or waiting by the PVC pipe, it might seem that the hatchery system wins. But that's not quite true. Because, across the country, more anglers value the wild trout. They're working to protect the wildness that remains, and reclaiming and restoring native trout to streams where they have not swum in decades or longer.

I suspect that one future for angling will feature banana trout on steroids, perhaps even with anglers lining up along concrete tanks to catch them. I suspect genetic engineering will deliver fishing scenarios beyond our wildest science fiction imagining. Some will go there, but it won't be the only option. I want to see a future for fishing where native trout have reclaimed their territories not only in national parks but even in the middle of cornfields.

The deification of trout, sure enough, got us into this mess. It led to concrete hatcheries and invasive species spilling into our waters. It led to banana trout. But the love of trout may, ultimately, help lead us to a better future.

CHAPTER TWO

The Ghosts of Cutthroats Past

Our little motor boat, filled with outdoor writers, bounced in the waves as gulls circled overhead. We approached the large boat as men in orange rain gear unfurled gillnets. The smells of fish and fuel already assaulted our nostrils. Pelicans followed the boat, waiting for the inevitable fish carcasses to fall overboard. It felt like a high-seas adventure, but we were in the middle of Yellowstone National Park.

The National Park Service was celebrating its 100th anniversary that summer. And I celebrated at our first national park—and one of my favorite places on Earth—on a commercial gillnetting boat. I admit: I'd rather be searching the valleys for wolves, or hiking among wildflowers, or, of course, casting dry flies to trout. This, though, was more important.

I came here to see the righting of a wrong, and one of the most ambitious native fish restoration efforts ever undertaken. Those gillnets were being deployed to kill as many invasive, non-native lake trout as possible, so that native Yellowstone cutthroat trout could hopefully return to their former glory.

I'm a child of "hook-and-bullet" magazines and outdoor books: those stories of adventure inspired in me a desire to see and experience the world's wild places. I created lists of where I wanted to go and things I wanted to do. One of those classic experiences was cutthroat trout fishing in the Yellowstone River. Every year, it seemed, there'd be another story of an angler catching dozens of cutthroats in an afternoon, all on dry flies. It seemed too good to be true. And it was.

By the time I first visited Yellowstone National Park in 2001, the Yellowstone River's cutthroat fishery was a pale shadow of its former self. Catching a single fish in an afternoon became an achievement. Few anglers lined the banks because the word was out: the cutthroats had essentially disappeared.

What had happened?

In 1994, a fishing boat on Yellowstone Lake reported an unusual catch: a lake trout. Lake trout are not native to Yellowstone, although they had been stocked in nearby Lewis Lake decades prior.

Exactly how they got there is unclear, and perhaps irrelevant. What soon became clear is the impact they would have on cutthroat trout, and an entire ecosystem. Yellowstone Lake is the largest body of water in the park. It also is connected to numerous rivers and streams, most notably the Yellowstone River. Cutthroat trout live in the lake and also migrate out to spawn each year. At one point, the population in this system numbered 3.5 million to 4 million trout: a highly productive fishery. And one of the best remaining strongholds for native, wild cutthroat.

Invasive lake trout found the conditions equally amenable. "One of the really hard things here is that this lake is really good lake trout habitat," says Pat Bigelow, National Park Service biologist. "Lake trout here have 2.5 times better survival than a typical, native lake trout population. They don't have any predators."

Biologists soon recognized the situation as dire: by the 2000s, the Yellowstone cutthroat population had declined by 95 percent.

This affected more than the storied sport fishing. Prone to cruising surface waters and shoals, cutthroat in the lake literally feed an ecosystem: grizzlies, ospreys, otters, and more dine on the trout as they move into feeder streams on their spawning run. The trout were highly migratory and could spawn as far as 30 or 40 miles from the lake—providing food for predators over a wide geographic area.

Lake trout, in contrast, spend much of their time in the lake's deep water—so they are not available to grizzlies and other predators. A key part of the ecosystem had been functionally eliminated. Looking out over the vastness of Yellowstone Lake, conservationists wondered: Was it already too late? Instead of wallowing in this despair, they launched an ambitious and perhaps even audacious plan to knock back the lake trout population.

The gillnetting boat we boarded that day had proven the most effective strategy in reducing the lake trout population. Using commercial fishing techniques in a national park in itself seems somewhat revolutionary.

"This is just one part of a park-wide program focused on native fish restoration and preservation," says Todd Koel, National Park Service biologist.

As we returned from our excursion, he pulled up a map outlining projects around the park aimed at bringing back fish including grayling, Westslope cutthroat trout, and other Yellowstone cutthroat trout populations. To a 21st-century conservationist, this might seem a given in our national parks. But it wasn't always that way.

In the early history of the national parks, managers often actively stocked non-native fish as part of their conservation program. At the time, it was believed that hatchery stocking helped sustain fish populations and fishing opportunities. Many anglers, often visitors from other parts of the country or world, wanted to catch fish species they were familiar with, and the Park Service was happy to oblige.

In the 1930s, some park biologists began arguing against stocking, but societal values were not there yet. The main goal was to provide fish for anglers to catch—and eat. According to Koel, it was not until the 1970s that park managers began aggressively promoting practices like catch and release, and attempting to preserve native fish. "It took a long time for the public to catch up," he says.

As he shared this history along the shores of Yellowstone Lake, an older man approached and began gesturing wildly. "The National Park Service could have avoided this whole situation if you had just killed the lake trout in Lewis Lake in the seventies," he said, referring to a lake where lake trout had been intentionally stocked in the earlier days of Yellowstone. "It was stupid. It's your fault. You could have stopped this."

Koel calmly replied, "We could have never convinced the public of that in the seventies, even if we had known the threat."

The man stormed off, still muttering about the folly of the Park Service. "It just shows the passion people have for native fish," says Dave Sweet, Yellowstone Lake special project manager for Trout Unlimited. "There are a lot of opinions, but people now care about the fate of native fish."

We can't go back decades and change past policy, values, and worldviews. But right here, right now, conservationists can make a difference in Yellowstone cutthroat restoration.

Five years ago, gillnetting boats launched onto Yellowstone Lake, plying the waters for lake trout. Biologists determined that only a large-scale effort could dent the invasive population, so just asking lake sport anglers to keep lake trout would never be sufficient.

The boats lay out miles of net at a time and pick them up three or four days later. They keep detailed records of the location and rate of catch, and that location helps direct where future efforts concentrate.

"This is science-based. But to work, sometimes it comes down to fishing sense," says Todd Koel. "It's knowing where to go, what tactics to use and recognizing that sometimes catching fish is just dumb luck."

The sustained effort has yielded significant numbers: more than 1.2 million lake trout have been removed to date, with insignificant bycatch of Yellowstone cutthroat.

The summer I visited, more than two hundred thousand lake trout had been removed by mid-July. As I stood on the boat, filled with the carcasses of more than 1,200 lake trout from just that morning, the challenge seemed overwhelming. The fishers removed nets filled with invasives, and the next day found even more invasives in their nets. It seemed the supply of lake trout was endless.

And that's part of the challenge: this isn't a short-term project. Biological models differ, predicting it could take between five and ten years for the lake trout population to be reduced to the point where the population crashes.

That requires money and resolve, and it's clear the National Park Service can't do it alone. The Yellowstone Park Foundation, Trout Unlimited, and other partners have pitched in to ensure that momentum keeps up.

"You can't make a five-year commitment to this and then say you're done," says Dan Wenk, then serving as Yellowstone National Park superintendent. "That would be throwing money away."

He pointed out that the seemingly never-ending commercial netting is not as bleak a task as it may appear. "Yes, we are seeing the same numbers, but we have to spend more effort to catch those same numbers of lake trout," he says.

In other words, the crews have to work harder to find the lake trout. But even if the gillnetting can crash the population, the work is not done.

"It's unlikely we'll ever be able to completely eliminate lake trout from Yellowstone Lake," Wenk says.

That means finding other ways to control the population. Trout Unlimited has funded tracking devices planted in lake trout so that biologists can see where they are spawning. The spawning beds, located in shallow lake waters, will be another focus of the control effort. Academic collaborators are helping devise effective techniques for killing eggs and making spawning sites unattractive. One bizarre strategy involves putting lake trout carcasses on spawning beds. The dead trout attract scavengers and make the spawning areas unviable for fish. (Lake trout carcasses are returned to the lake. While some believe this is wasteful, it is keeping the nutrients of the fish bodies in the ecosystem.)

While full restoration may seem a long way off, lately it's hard to miss some promising signs. Fishing guides have begun posting videos from wilderness tributaries of Yellowstone Lake, showing clients catching cutthroats of significant size. For years, many outfitters didn't offer these trips due to a lack of fish. Grizzlies show up at Yellowstone Lake tributaries in the spring for what had been a reliable source of protein in the form of migrating and spawning cutthroat. The bears left with empty stomachs over the past decade, but have found the fish again thanks to the netting efforts.

Since my trip, the boats continue to ply the waters. They're still catching thousands of lake trout, and there are still hopeful signs. But it's also clear that, if the gillnetting were to stop, the lake trout population would be back to its former levels in a year or two.

Around the West, so many cutthroat trout stories mirror what happened in Yellowstone Lake. Or worse. These beautiful, native, perfectly adapted fish have not fared well in modern times. In some streams, overharvest or dams or improper cattle grazing have hurt. But mostly, once again, their fate has been determined by invasive species.

As the late Robert Behnke, the preeminent expert on trout and salmon in North America, put it,

> *The most significant aspect of cutthroat trout life history, ecology and biology that can be offered to explain their great decline in distribution and abundance concerns the cutthroat trout's susceptibility to hybridization with rainbow trout and to replacement by brown trout and brook trout in streams and by lake trout in large lakes.*

Cutthroat trout evolved into distinct subspecies in isolated mountain ranges around the West. Biologists have typically recognized twelve to fourteen subspecies, of which two are extinct and most are imperiled. In a recurring theme for many freshwater fish, biologists are just learning the real diversity, and there will likely be more recognized subspecies soon.

All cutthroats have the characteristic red slash on the bottom edge of their jaw that gives them their name. But each subspecies has different colorations and spotting patterns, and are found in wildly varying habitats. Sea-run cutthroats migrate from the sea to spawn in freshwater habitats, just like steelhead and salmon. Other subspecies move from lakes to small streams, or large rivers to small streams. Still others are resident year-round in the same habitat.

All this diversity, almost lost to fish stocking fervor. At one point, anglers derided cutthroat trout as too easy to catch and too sluggish on the line. Lately, though, more and more anglers value the native diversity. For an angler-naturalist, pursuing the different subspecies in their native ranges is a bucket-list worthy challenge. That interest is fueling restoration across the Western United States. While it indeed was anglers who caused this situation, anglers now lead the charge to return cutthroats.

The methods vary by habitat, by practicality, by funding, and by political will. In some streams, conservationists have killed the non-native fish through rotenone, a fish-killing pesticide, and then restocked with native species. The South Fork of the Snake River has regulations that encourage anglers to kill non-native rainbow trout, even providing financial incentives. The coldwater conservation group Trout Unlimited has led the charge in restoring native trout. Right now, according to the organization's president and CEO, Chris Wood, a lot of the organization's efforts are aimed at making sure streams within cutthroat trout range are connected and not blocked by dams, roads, or other barriers.

"These fish need to be able to exhibit their full life histories. They need to be able to reach their spawning grounds," he says.

"Reconnected waters allow fish to better adapt to floods and fire and drought. That's what we need for long-term conservation of native fishes."

In the past year, Trout Unlimited projects reconnected about 770 miles of streams that had been inaccessible to native fish. Angler interest in cutthroat trout continues to grow. Despite that good work, many cutthroat subspecies can only be found in 10 percent of their historic waters. At times, chasing cutthroats today can feel a bit like chasing ghosts.

∼

Elk bugles sounded across the meadow as my colleague, Tyler Johnson, and I donned daypacks at the trailhead. Visitors lined the nearby roads, taking pictures of the grazing elk herds and the jaw-dropping scenery. We, too, stopped to enjoy both, but we had cutthroat trout to meet, and some hard miles to get there.

We were at Colorado's Rocky Mountain National Park, one of the prettier places on the continent, and also one of the better places to catch a cutthroat. It also happened to be Tyler's backyard, so he knew the perfect alpine lake to visit.

As soon as we strapped on packs, he began bounding up the trail. One of Tyler's favorite pastimes is an event called the Flyathlon, which combines competitive trail racing, fly fishing, and craft beer drinking. He also backpacks solo on wilderness elk hunts. As he galloped up the trail, I was glad I had recently run a half-marathon, so I could at least pretend to keep up. Still, I found myself sucking wind in the high, alpine elevations.

We hiked switchbacks for a couple of hours, slowly gaining elevation. Finally, a little wooden sign announced we had arrived at our lake, sitting at 9,500 feet. It sat like a bowl, surrounded by snow-capped mountain slopes and granite. Postcard worthy. Worth the hike on its own. Find wild cutthroat trout, and you'll find gorgeous places.

A couple of anglers had beaten us there, so we went to the opposite side of the lake. A couple of rises pocked the surface in the middle of the lake. I noted a pod of fish cruising the shallows. We began stringing our fly rods.

A half hour later, the fish had studiously ignored our big, hairy dry flies. There's a fair amount in the angling literature about how "unselective" cutthroat trout are, as if this was a character flaw. In a high mountain stream, food is sparse enough that native trout can't afford to be selective. They also have less contact with humans.

If cutthroat trout see a lot of artificial flies, they, too, become wary. It appeared the lake before us got plenty of fishing pressure due to the high volume of national park visitors. Tyler switched to a tiny midge fly, and quickly had a trout on. I changed to my go-to fly, a small pheasant tail nymph, and cast out to three trout cruising the shoreline. This time, the cutthroat didn't hesitate. It slurped up the nymph, and after a short fight, I had the fish along the bank.

Its sides shined bright red in the sun, set off nicely from its dark back. I slipped it back into the lake.

The day proceeded along similar lines. The fishing never got hot. One of us would catch a fish or two, then nothing for a half hour. I slowly moved around the lake, watching for fish and enjoying the surrounds. I noticed fish beginning to rise a long cast from shore. Even better, the trees lining the lake opened up in that area, allowing for a long backcast. I tied on a dry fly, put out line, and immediately saw a subtle dimple right where my fly landed. I set the hook. For fifteen minutes, I enjoyed the perfect spot, reeling in several fish that attacked my dry flies. Each was bright and colorful. Wild.

But these fish had their own weird story. The trout before me were lost, seemingly forever, and then found, a dramatic story of native fish resurrection. Or so everyone thought.

❧

The greenback cutthroat trout, a subspecies found only in Colorado, was declared extinct in 1937, gone forever due to the usual list of factors. At least it appeared that way. In the 1950s, fisheries managers found greenbacks holding on in a remote reach of Rocky Mountain National Park, the same park I fished. At the time, there was little will or legal muscle to pursue conservation. When the Endangered Species Act passed in 1973, greenback cutthroat trout were on the list. That began an effort to gather some of the survivors and propagate them in hatcheries for reintroduction into other waters.

By just about any measure, that effort proved spectacularly successful. The fish were widely reintroduced, and they prospered, including in the lake where I fished with Tyler. By the late 1990s, they were recognized as a model for endangered species recovery.

In native fish conservation, declaring "mission accomplished" can always be risky. In this case, the fish continued to prosper, but scientific advances in the form of genetic testing proved to be a major buzz kill. Most of the "greenback" cutthroat trout, it turned out, were not genetically pure. In 1999, the University of Colorado conducted genetic tests that confirmed that most of the fish stocked were not what they first appeared. This led to a renewed and more careful effort to stock only pure greenbacks. In 2007, in another blow, it was discovered that these "pure" greenbacks now being used for conservation stocking, were, in fact, another subspecies: Colorado River cutthroats. This subspecies is beautiful in its own right and has also been eliminated from much of its native habitat. But Colorado River cutthroats are not as rare as greenbacks.

Why were they misidentified? For one thing, they look somewhat similar. At the time of their "rediscovery," no one had seen a live greenback cutt for decades. And fish stocking also played a surprising role. It's believed that early fish stockers put Colorado River cutthroat trout in waters formerly occupied by greenbacks. They didn't exactly thrive, but they held on, and when fish biologists found them, they assumed they were the native subspecies based on range.

At one point, an angler fishing in this same lake would have ticked "greenback cutthroat trout" off his angling life list. By the time I fished there, some anglers still insisted these fish were greenbacks. But the genetics was clear: these were Colorado River cutthroat trout.

There's another twist to this story. In the late 1800s, a homesteader named Joseph C. Jones stocked trout near his new home on Bear Creek, near Pike's Peak. Some have surmised that he did this to attract tourists to a planned lodge facility, but his exact motivations remain unclear. However, these stocked fish proved to indeed be genetically pure greenback cutthroat trout, protected from hybridization by barriers downriver. In 2007, the seven-hundred-fish population in Bear Creek was likely the only genetically pure cutthroat trout remaining.

Ironically, they were outside their historic range. Jones had introduced a non-native fish to his stream and, in doing so, saved it from extinction.

That's the popular current narrative, at least. Given the cutthroat populations already lost, some wonder whether we can ever completely understand the historic variability of subspecies and strains. The late Robert Behnke believed the efforts to distinguish greenbacks from Colorado River cutthroats were misplaced. As he described to writer Ted Williams:

> When once widely distributed subspecies such as the greenback and Colorado River cutthroat trout are fragmented into tiny, isolated populations as they are today, genetic analysis will give incomplete and uncertain results. Natural genetic variation once widespread in the ancestor that gave rise to small, isolated populations was wrongly interpreted as evidence of hybridization. . . . I expressed my opinion that to get the recovery efforts back on track, it must be simplified and realistically evaluated in the light of the uncertainty of genetic data. If it looks like a duck, walks like a duck, and quacks like a duck, we should call it a duck. Getting into the molecular structure of a duck can result in confusion and chaos. Now substitute greenback cutthroat trout for duck, and move on.

The saga to restore cutthroat trout is a tangled web indeed. Similar stories play out for other cutthroat trout subspecies around the West. Untangling the genetics, of what fish belongs where, can seem hopeless, especially when early stocking was so random, and the understanding of stream ecology so poor.

———

Does any of this matter? Even to many conservation-minded anglers, "a cutthroat is a cutthroat is a cutthroat." Is it worth the money, effort, and inevitable setbacks to try to restore native subspecies and strains?

For some of us, the answer is a clear "yes." Perhaps it's as simple as Aldo Leopold's "refined taste in natural objects." Or perhaps the variety of trout colors and shapes makes fishing more fun.

Whatever the case, one thing is clear: it's difficult to see a path forward for cutthroat trout conservation, for native fish conservation, without angler support. Conservation writer Ted Williams has noted that much of the public doesn't consider fish to be wildlife: if they care at all, fish are something for dinner plates and aquariums. So it comes down to people who fish. How do they get more involved?

Enter the Cutthroat Slam. Sportsmen have long been fond of "slams," catching (or shooting) a certain number of species for either a formal or informal award. It began with legendary outdoor writer Jack O'Connor, who wrote about the bagging of North America's main four sheep species and subspecies as a "Grand Slam." Since then, there have been slams created for everything from wild turkey subspecies to billfish.

Wyoming created a Cutthroat Slam twenty-four years ago, with a certificate going to any angler who caught (and sent photos) of the state's four native cutthroat subspecies. My friend Brett Prettyman, who for twenty-five years was an outdoor writer for the *Salt Lake Tribune*, thought the idea could work in Utah, but the Utah Department of Wildlife Resources staff thought there wouldn't be enough interest. After all, states like Nevada struggled to attract any participants to their native fish award program.

When Prettyman left the newspaper for Trout Unlimited, he saw an opportunity to revisit the Utah Cutthroat Slam—with a twist. Trout Unlimited would partner with the state agency. Anglers would pay up front to participate, enrolling them in the slam program. If they caught Utah's four subspecies, they got a medallion. The money raised would go to cutthroat conservation and restoration projects.

With Trout Unlimited's ability to market the program, it quickly took off. Prettyman runs Utah Cutthroat Slam social media, and every trout caught for the slam gets featured. To date, 1,206 anglers have signed on, with 234 completing the slam (two over-achievers have done it six times each).

"This isn't just for fly fishing," says Prettyman. "Anglers just need to follow the rules of whatever water they're on. It's an excuse to go to awesome, new places with family and friends, a chance to explore parts of the state many would never visit otherwise."

Many conservationists believe that education means lectures and fact sheets. But Prettyman sees another kind of education with the slam. "One of the requirements is that the subspecies must be caught in its native range," he says. "We have anglers posting photos and asking if it's native. They've accidentally learned something—and they liked that they learned it. People are proud to know more about the fish."

The part I love about Utah's program is the conservation component. It isn't just about fishing achievement; by pursuing cutthroat trout, anglers are ensuring that these trout can be restored to more stream miles. For instance, the upper Weber River was cut off to spawning Bear River cutthroat trout for fifty years due to a cement barrier installed underneath an interstate. The Cutthroat Slam funding helped install fish ladders, opening up miles of river to native fish. Prettyman was there when the ladders were installed.

"A woman stopped and literally had tears in her eyes," he said. "She said she hadn't seen cutthroats in the river since she was a little girl. It is really rewarding to see conservation in action."

So many of the cutthroat trout stories are about returning what's been lost, about righting past wrongs. My first encounter with wild cutts, when my wife and I moved to Idaho seventeen years ago, was not like this.

Our first night, we camped along a little stream in Bear Valley, in the vast national forestland of Central Idaho. There was still a little light left after we pitched our tent, so I walked down to the water and began casting flies. Suddenly, a giant form tore up through the stream, sending a huge wake. Frankly, it didn't compute. I had never seen a trout this big. In fact, I was pretty sure that trout *couldn't* get so big in such a small stream.

The next day, I realized I was correct in this. It wasn't a trout. We drove to Dagger Falls, on the edge of the Frank Church River of No Return Wilderness, one of the country's largest and most storied wild places. We stopped to look at the falls, and suddenly noticed large fish jumping up them: Chinook salmon. That large form the night before was a salmon setting up a spawning bed.

We hiked into the wilderness and soon noticed finger-sized salmonflies—a large species of stonefly—gathering along the banks. Periodically, they'd fly and touch down on the water . . . and fish would dart to the surface and gulp them in savage, predatory lunges. I fumbled through my fly boxes, and tied on the biggest, gaudiest flies I could find. And the fish—Westslope cutthroat trout—attacked these with equal gusto.

No one questioned what subspecies these were. Fishing here was not chasing ghosts. These fish had remained, and prospered. And that isn't an accident. The secret ingredient at work here is the very foundation of native fish conservation and, I believe, the future of quality fishing. Wild fish and wild fishing thrive where there are ample public lands. It's as simple as that.

"Without public lands, native fish conservation is over," says Trout Unlimited's Chris Wood. "It's the whole game. Period. All the native fish species of the Western United States are dependent on wilderness-quality public lands."

When we speak, Woods quickly reels off the importance of roadless lands to Idaho's native fish: 68 percent of the remaining bull trout, 74 percent of the Chinook salmon and steelhead, and 58 percent of the Westslope cutthroat trout are found in roadless areas.

He says it again, for emphasis: "You simply cannot protect these fish if you don't have public lands. High-quality public lands."

When I stand on a mountain top in Idaho, the public lands—our lands—stretch out as far as the eye can see. And the large, unbroken landscapes are what are going to allow native fish to survive even apocalyptic conditions. Research has shown that climate change will have dire consequences for native trout, including cutthroats. An article in the *Proceedings of the National Academy of Sciences* (PNAS) by Trout Unlimited's Seth J. Wenger and other coauthors projected that cutthroat trout will lose 58 percent of their habitat by 2080. The only real hope for these fish is expansive, public lands. US Forest Service researcher Dan Isaak found that cutthroat trout and bull trout will not be as hard hit as many believe in places like Idaho. That's because Idaho still has huge tracts of national forest with free-flowing rivers. The extensive, connected rivers found on public lands allow trout to move higher in altitude, into cooler stretches of stream, without seriously impacting their overall population.

That assumes, of course, that public lands remain public. And that's a big assumption these days. Many vocal legislators and lobbyists have begun agitating for "state control" of public lands, even though the states have scant resources to manage them. Others are more forthright: they just want them sold to the highest bidder in a libertarian frenzy.

Chris Wood has been involved in these issues for decades, beginning from when he worked for Mike Dombeck, head of the

Forest Service under President Clinton. Dombeck had proposed protection for 60 million acres of remaining roadless areas under the Roadless Area Conservation Rule.

"I was sent out to communicate with constituents, mainly those that Mike thought were too controversial," Wood says with a laugh. "I met with mining companies, timber companies and ranchers. And on the other side, I met with a lot of environmentalists. But in those years, I never got a request for a meeting from the hunting and fishing community. They had the most to gain or lose. But they weren't involved."

When Wood came to work for Trout Unlimited, he wanted to change that. The organization launched the Public Lands Initiative (now called the Sportsmen's Conservation Project). While many organizations launching outreach campaigns hire lobbyists who thrive in Beltway politics or marketers who create slick ads, Trout Unlimited recruited outdoor writers who had serious sporting and wilderness experience. People like my friend Scott Stouder, one of the toughest outdoorsmen I know, someone who is quite comfortable packing into the wilderness and hunting elk for weeks on end.

Other organizations have joined the fight, most notably the Backcountry Hunters and Anglers. In recent years, as the threat to public lands has become more visible, that organization's membership doubled. Still, too many sportsmen take these lands for granted. Many don't realize the wealth they have. Many see laws they don't like, or see federal mismanagement of lands, and think the state could do better.

When I'm casting on a stream, watching a cutthroat torpedo out of the water for a dry fly, I can only marvel that we still have this freedom. Freedom to fish, yes. But also the freedom to restore, to reintroduce, to experiment. While the nuances of cutthroat trout conservation—really, of all conservation—may be complicated, or just downright messy, it's still possible. Climate change and invasive species present major obstacles. But we can still have a future with cutthroat trout—as long as there are public lands and waters. And as long as there are anglers fighting for both the fish and the rivers they call home.

Chapter Three

Gila Trout Burning

The last time I'd set foot in Gila National Forest, my quest proved futile. My dad and I had joined my cousin David and Uncle Bill to hunt for javelina, the small, pig-like hoofed mammals that aren't really pigs. When we pulled into our cabin, the manager came out to greet us and show us around.

"I don't want anyone shooting around the ranch, because I still keep livestock," she said. "But there are some good spots not too far away for quail or deer."

"We're hunting javelinas," I said.

"Oh, in that case, you can hunt around the ranch as much as you want," she said.

I at first took that to mean she had a dislike of javelinas. I later realized it was because she recognized we wouldn't be shooting. The next morning, hunting an area suggested by one of my cousin's friends, I ran into a birder, who told me he had been coming to this spot for eighteen years and had never seen a javelina. By day two, it became apparent that the nearest javelina likely resided 50 miles away. By day three, all involved realized that the probability of finding a javelina was more or less the same as finding Bigfoot. It's often said that you don't have to get anything to have a good time hunting or fishing. This is true, but of course an important disclaimer is that it sure helps to at least have a *chance* of getting something. Nonetheless, we played gin rummy, visited cliff dwellings, and made the best of it.

I hoped for better luck this time around, when I came to catch the native Gila trout. Initial signs weren't necessarily promising. At a conservation fundraising banquet, I had bid on a trip to fish for Gila trout in Arizona, just across the border from my failed javelina hunt. It wasn't a guided trip; organizational members took you out for an experience in their backyards.

When I won the bid, it took me several weeks of emails and phone messages just to reach the person who would take me fishing. It turned out that others had volunteered him, and he seemed confused by my request. The trip was scheduled for summer, but he said that was not a good time for native trout fishing. He would be available in March, if I didn't mind camping in snow drifts. I didn't, although that seemed an odd time for Gila trout. I inquired about this.

"The one stream in Arizona with Gila trout is closed to fishing, due to fires," he said.

I let the organization keep the bid as a donation but canceled the trip. As I researched Gila trout, online sources seemed contradictory and discouraging. This native trout had been reintroduced to a number of streams and rivers in the Gila National Forest, but a series of forest fires had wiped out much of the recovery effort. Matthew Dickinson's *Trout in the Desert* concluded with a lengthy wilderness search for Gila trout. The author failed to catch one.

I started to write off my chances at a Gila trout, when Jason Amaro, the New Mexico representative for Backcountry Hunters and Anglers, suggested I meet him at a creek that he assured me had good fishing for Gilas in the summer. I signed on. On a warm August evening, I drove into Reserve, New Mexico, with a billboard that read, "BEWARE—DANGER. Free Roaming Wolves. Protect Your Children & Your Pets." It featured gory photos of a ripped-up and very dead calf, and a hound with shredded ears.

Reserve is located in Catron County, the largest county in New Mexico with its third-lowest population. It is often noted for a county ordinance suggesting that every household contain a firearm, often misrepresented in the press trying to portray this community as a last bastion of gunslingers. Nonetheless, the small main street had a distinctly Old West feel including a prominent statue of a gunfighter, pistol drawn.

I pulled into a little diner and was promptly served two burritos in a searing red chili sauce. The waitress had a raspy smoker's voice and assured me this was the best burrito in Catron County. When I asked for directions to my hotel, located a few miles outside town, she admitted she had only lived in Reserve a few months.

"I came here to get away from a bad situation," she said. "And you can never get too far away from a bad situation, but this is pretty darn close."

Even this far, even in the nearby wilderness that Aldo Leopold made famous, non-native trout had replaced the natives. A considerable effort to replace the exotics with native Gila trout was underway, but it seemed the effort kept hitting obstacles.

The next morning, I drove out of Reserve, and wondered if I'd find the fish. I quickly entered the national forest and, despite the stunning scenery, felt an uncharacteristic gloom. This became even more pronounced when I followed my GPS up a mountain road that looked like little more than two tracks cut in rocks. As I bottomed out and drove over jagged boulders, I wondered if my Gila trout trip might end right here. How many times had I ridiculed people who trusted their GPS over common sense? I got to the top of the mountain and saw three elk guides, scouting with scopes. They had driven up in ATVs.

"You brought that up here?" one asked.

"It's a rental car," I replied. The three guides glanced at each other.

I asked for directions to my campground meeting spot, and one replied, "You should have taken the nice gravel road all the way in. You chose the worst road in this county. And if you haven't figured it out yet, this is a big county, with a lot of bad roads."

I asked what my prognosis was for getting off the mountain with rental car more or less intact. "You made it this far," one replied. "I don't think much of anything from here on out is going to give you trouble."

The downhill descent proved relatively smooth. Coming off the mountain with only a small chip in the windshield seemed a minor victory. I drove on to the campsite where Amaro suggested meeting. He texted me a few nights before that he might be running late, and to just start fishing without him. "Just look for a short, round Mexican," he wrote. I saw no one fitting that description, so I decided to start off on my own. I knew biologists had successfully removed all rainbow and brown trout from this stretch of stream, but I suspected the Gilas were only in the headwaters. Most Gila trout trip reports involve lengthy backcountry hikes, if not horseback rides.

A guy saddling a horse in the parking lot changed my plans. "You fishing for those Gila trout?" he asked, looking at my fly rod.

I nodded and asked him how long a hike I needed to make.

"Oh, just head down the hill here, and start fishing in the big hole. Right here in the campground. You'll catch all you want," he said.

I thanked him and carried my little three-weight to the stream. It's rare that I've found good fishing adjacent to popular camp sites. I made a couple of casts as soon as I got to the stream, but the habitat didn't look promising. I bushwhacked through thick vegetation and came to a deep but narrow hole. I cast, mended, and rolled out another loop of line.

My dry fly floated on the surface, and suddenly a little trout darted out of the depths and smacked it. It darted back down, sans fly, but I smiled. Could it really be that easy?

Yes. The next cast, I had my first Gila trout on, a lovely, golden little thing, reminiscent of a rainbow trout that spent too much time in a tanning parlor. Then I caught three more out of the same hole. There would be no suspense, no drama, no quixotic quest. The way, really, native trout fishing should be.

⟶ ⟵

Like native cutthroat trout, Gila trout were hit hard by non-native fish introductions; rainbow trout hybridize readily with Gilas. By the 1950s, Gila trout existed in only five New Mexico streams, all in remote wilderness areas. The New Mexico Game and Fish Department had recognized the fish's plight even before that and had stopped stocking non-native trout in Gila trout waters, and had prohibited fishing for Gilas.

The trout made the first listing of the federal Endangered Species Act in 1973, launching further efforts to protect and restore the fish. But the fact that you couldn't fish for Gila trout made angler support tough to come by.

"We would remove non-native trout and reintroduce Gila trout, and we'd have to close the stream to all fishing," says Jill Wick, Gila trout biologist for the New Mexico Department of Fish and Game. "The public simply saw this as losing a place to go fishing."

In 2006, enough progress had been made in Gila trout recovery to upgrade the species to Threatened status. This initiated the Gila Trout Recovery Plan, which laid out specific goals for restoration. A state-of-the-art hatchery bred fish to survive in wild conditions, and breeding was carefully conducted to promote genetic diversity. The lineages of the trout from each of the remaining streams with pure Gila trout have been preserved.

An equally important part of the plan was that it allowed recreational angling. Most streams where Gila trout were reintroduced were off limits to angling, but select streams did allow fishing. Excess hatchery fish were also stocked in lakes and less-pristine streams, allowing for a put-and-take fishery. Now Gila trout were not an off-limits endangered species; they were something you could catch.

"Recreational angling has become a really important part of the conservation and recovery program," says Wick. "We can rally a lot of support for Gila trout."

Gila trout became established in eighteen streams, but then calamity arrived in another form: fire. In 2012, the Whitewater-Baldy Fire became the largest fire in New Mexico history, burning 300,000 acres of forest. The fires occurred just before the annual monsoon rains, which put out the fire but also sent a thick layer of ash into streams, literally choking all fish in them.

Fire is a natural part of the ecosystem, of course, but decades of fire suppression and climate change have changed the pattern and intensity. Gila trout, also, were found in many more streams. "Historically, even if a fire had burned and wiped out trout in a stream, other trout would have just moved in from another stream," says Wick. "Now, we don't have that connectivity."

Six of the eighteen streams with Gila trout lost all their fish. In some streams, Gila trout were evacuated to preserve their genetics. Prior to the fire, the Gila trout recovery effort had rightly been hailed as a stunning success. But the quick loss of so many trout populations cast a damper. The uncertainty of climate change—with the potential for changes to fire cycles, precipitation levels, and water temperatures—makes the future for Gila trout far from certain.

But as bad as the Whitewater-Baldy Fire was, there were silver linings. I was benefiting from one of those, on Willow Creek.

—◦—

I continued fishing, catching fish out of each deep pool I encountered. I admit I was lost in the reverie of dry fly fishing at its finest when I heard a whoop. I looked up and saw an energetic man bounding toward me. Jason Amaro.

"I see you didn't have trouble catching fish," says Amaro. "And I bet you want to catch a few more. Let's meet at the parking lot in an hour or so."

I continued fishing, catching a few more trout, and then made my way to our meeting spot. Amaro suggested we walk downstream to see the reason for this stellar fishing. We walked a little footpath until suddenly a large, cement dam appeared in the middle of the stream. It looked brand new, blocky, imposing. In the midst of all this wildness, it felt like an intrusion, but looks can be deceiving.

Willow Creek did not have Gila trout when the Whitewater-Baldy Fire hit. It contained a population of brown trout that outcompete and even eat Gila trout. After the fire, the toxic ash wiped the stream clear of brown trout. Repeated electrofishing efforts failed to turn up any fish. The fire, essentially, had cleared Willow Creek for a native fish recovery.

The one problem was that Willow Creek, like any creek, is connected to other waters—waters that still had non-native fish. So conservationists installed a barrier making the upstream inaccessible to non-native fish, a tactic increasingly used to protect native trout throughout the West. The same features that make dams so hated by fish conservationists, in this case, became the dam's selling point.

A dam is not without downsides, as Trout Unlimited's senior scientist, Helen Neville, points out. "A dam like this is necessary for streams like Willow, threatened by non-native species. But these small fragmented populations are, in the long term, at greater risk of extinction from isolation, and will require active management to replace lost fish and restore genetic diversity," she writes.

The barrier on Willow was installed and Gila trout were stocked upstream. "If the fish have just a bit of structure, a bit of food, they thrive," says Amaro. "The habitat is here. After we introduced the fish, they were spawning the next year."

The stream was soon open to fishing, making it one of the most accessible Gila trout streams. "Not everyone can go deep into the wilderness," says Amaro. "You don't need to take a horseback trip to catch this fish. It isn't just a mythical fish off limits to all but the hardiest anglers. You can catch one, right here."

And that's been a part of Amaro's mission, one shared by others passionate about Gila trout conservation: to introduce anglers to the fish. The New Mexico Department of Fish and Game offers excellent resources pointing anglers to the best streams. They recognize that keeping Gila trout locations carefully guarded secrets does not ultimately help the fish.

"I don't even fish for them anymore," says Amaro. "I just bring people here to share the experience. I take a sense of ownership. And I don't see any way to recovery without support from sportsmen."

I cast out a fly below the dam but didn't have any takes. Amaro, meanwhile, pulled out sandwiches with all the fixings, chips, and sodas for a streamside lunch. I commented on the oddity of enjoying a lunch in such a wild space by a concrete structure.

"The wilderness is why we still have Gila trout," Amaro said. "It can also make some of the management difficult. You can't use motors in the wilderness. It's difficult to access. But if we're going to save this fish, we're going to have to accept some active management."

After lunch, I headed back up river. I made my way through some willows and found a deep hole I hadn't previously fished. The tight cover required me to dap my fly right off my rod tip. An eager Gila trout immediately engulfed it.

Was the experience altered by the presence of a cement dam a half mile downstream? Did it make this native trout fishing any less fulfilling?

It struck me that I was in the wilderness that helped shape the philosophy of one of my heroes, Aldo Leopold. Like so many conservationists, I read his words young, I read them often, I quoted them and pondered over them. He recognized the need for civilized people to have wild country. One of his most quoted lines is, "What avail are *forty freedoms* without a blank spot on the map?"

Never in history are those blank spots so important, so valuable. Places where people can get lost, where wild things can survive without their every move monitored, are likely necessary for our collective sanity. But we can't let purity standards for wilderness wipe out the wild.

A lot of wilderness defenders I know bristle at the ideas of so-called eco-modernists, who believe that wilderness is nothing but a construct, that all of the earth is impacted by humanity, and that we better start behaving that way. Prominent eco-modernist Emma Marris has come under fire from environmentalists for suggesting that the earth be approached like a garden (a *rambunctious garden*, as her book is titled), with humans tending the entirety of the planet. This prompted conservation biologist Edward O. Wilson to ask, "Where do you plant that white flag you're carrying?"

I don't want every acre of every wild place to be monitored, managed, documented, and measured. Nor do I want every wild creature to be radio-tagged, tracked, and patrolled. It's a depressing future.

But what about these Gila trout? Is a cement barrier that big a price to pay to restore the native inhabitants to the stream? Isn't Willow Creek more natural now, overall, than if it only contained European brown trout?

The lines become blurry, but I'll take the native fish. I want there to be as little human influence as possible in the Gila wilderness, but we're going to have to make decisions: based on fires, on climate change, on non-native species. A hands-off approach will not save the wilderness from humanity. And we certainly wouldn't have Gila trout.

I cast again, and immediately hooked up with another feisty little fish. I take heart that they're still here. The ill-conceived fish stocking of the past and a hellish fire ultimately proved no match for the ingenuity and dedication of native fish advocates.

I sneaked along the stream, coming to a deep side pocket shaded by vegetation. I made a lousy cast, and gently pulled my fly back to prepare for a roll cast. As I did, I saw at least three Gila trout swirl around it on the surface. Such abundance . . . as if this place was untouched, as if these fish had never left.

CHAPTER FOUR

Trout of the Corn

Comedian and songwriter Heywood Banks sings a ditty called "Interstate 80 Iowa" intended to be an audio tour of, as he puts it, "one of the scenic highways of America." It basically consists of him singing the word "corn" over and over, interspersed occasionally with a city or tree sighting. It's actually not too far off the mark: Iowa has arguably lost more of its natural habitat than any other state, and that's in no small part due to King Corn.

More than 99 percent of the original prairie is gone. The state ranks forty-ninth in public land access. The environmental issue dominating the Iowa news lately, though, is the impact of intensive agriculture on the state's rivers and streams. Many fields contain tiles, essentially drains to pipe water away to keep crops from flooding. Those tiles dump water, now carrying fertilizers and pesticides, directly into streams. The city of Des Moines spent $900,000 in 2013 for nitrate removal; according to a story in *Politico*, it would cost $80 million to update its nitrate removal system sufficiently to protect water users. That led Des Moines Water Works to sue three rural counties for water pollution. While many farmers are adopting voluntary conservation measures, water quality remains a contentious issue.

Pondering over those cornfields, you could be forgiven if you think this is one of the last places you should go trout fishing.

But if you're able to drive a bit off the interstate, and put your preconceived notions aside, what you find may surprise you. In fact, Iowa's fisheries management suggests that, even in a place of intensive agriculture, we can still protect and restore native trout.

⚊ ⚊

Rolling hills stretched out before me, and while there was plenty of corn, the topography revealed small pastures, woodlands, even limestone bluffs. Farming was still visibly the dominant land use, but this would never be confused with the endless, flat cornfields fit for a comedic song. Much of the agricultural Midwest achieved its legendary flatness courtesy of the Ice Age, when glaciers scoured rocks away. But those glaciers never covered parts of Wisconsin, Minnesota, northwestern Illinois, or northeastern Iowa: a region known as the Driftless area. You can still sit on limestone bluffs and watch bald eagles soar overhead. You might find ancient American Indian mounds, built for ceremonial purposes. In the spring woods, you can seek tasty morel mushrooms by fallen trees, turkey gobbles rumbling in the background.

I've become familiar with this landscape, because this northeast corner of Iowa is where my wife Jennifer grew up on a farm. On this fine summer day, I joined her younger brother, Doug Puffett—the fifth generation to farm this land—on a trout-fishing expedition. He had promised our two nieces, Samantha and Kelli, a day out on the water as he could not take them a previous weekend.

For most of its existence, the Puffett Farm has been a dairy operation. Unlike the modern, confined dairies that often have thousands of cows, this one never had much more than a hundred (and often less). But the work never ended; on our visits, I'd hear Jennifer's father up before dawn, out to milk the cows—a process to be repeated again in the evening. In between came the daily battle of overcoming problems with machinery, crops, animals, and bills.

A few years ago, Doug and Jennifer's dad had transitioned out of the dairy business, now focusing on beef and crops. But it's still a daunting work load. Between the farm, kids, church, and the school board, Doug isn't exactly swimming in free time. Fishing isn't really a hobby so much as an occasional fun outing to enjoy with family.

As was the case on this particular day. We drove to the nearby Big Springs Hatchery, a state facility that included camping, river access, and two ponds set aside for youngsters only. The ponds, according to Doug, were almost always stocked full of rainbow trout. He warned that Kelli and Samantha, ages five and eight, wouldn't have very long attention spans, so we needed some place to catch fish quickly.

We got to the pond and indeed found rainbows circling around the surface of the first pond. Doug already had the rods rigged, so we quickly baited them with worms. The girls already wandered away.

"Stay away from the bank; it's slick there," Doug warned.

Two seconds later: "Get away from the bank. You're going to fall in."

He began a third warning, but he barely got "away" out when Samantha toppled over the ledge. She shrieked as she sank to her waist in the pond. We quickly grasped her arm and pulled her out. She screamed and cried.

"Do you believe me now?" Doug asked. She nodded her head as her body convulsed with sobs.

"Let's catch a fish and you'll forget about it," he said. Samantha took a rod and whipped out a cast that went maybe 5 feet. It scarcely mattered as the worm was immediately mobbed by trout. Samantha pulled too soon, and the trout darted away. But one swung back and engulfed the worm. She began reeling furiously, and the trout flopped on the bank.

Now she squealed with delight, even as she yelled, "It's gross," and, then, "Kill it." Doug obliged, dumping it in our bucket.

With Samantha on the board, Kelli fidgeted a bit. "I want to catch one, Uncle Matt," she said. We walked to the other side of the pond, to give a little casting room. I helped and her bobber landed with a plop. Samantha squealed again; she was on the verge of catching her second trout, filling her pond limit.

"I'm not going to get one," Kelli said.

I urged her to give it a minute.

"I don't like this spot."

I said we could move, in a minute.

"I don't like fishing."

And then, the bobber plunged. She continued her list of grievances against fishing, unaware of what lurked at the end of her line. I began barking at her to reel. She suddenly realized she had one on. "Help me, Uncle Matt! Don't let it go!"

At this point, I became as frantic about losing this fish as she was and just blurted, "Reel, reel, REEL!" And she did. The fish got caught in some reeds, but I leaned down and pulled it out.

"Uncle Matt, I love fishing!" Kelli exclaimed. "I want to go fishing every day with you."

She kept happily talking the whole way back to the farm. And on days like that, I have to brush my disdain for the hatchery system aside. Not every fishing trip has to be expeditionary, and not every angler has to make it a "lifestyle." Maybe some of those young anglers at the pond will indeed love it so much they want to go every day, leading them to wilder rivers and wilder fish.

I also realized that if many anglers thought about Iowa trout fishing at all, it would be a scene like this they envisioned. In an area dominated by farms, the only thing left would be trout ponds. But the limestone country of the Driftless area contained more secrets.

———

I wiped sweat from my brow, as Bill Green stopped ahead of me. "You know where we are?" he asked.

I shook my head. He seemed pleased by the answer. Bill, who attended church with my in-laws, invited me to fish one of his secret spots. One of the ways he ensures his spots remain secret is to take any guest via the longest distance between two points, a distance that invariably involves bushwhacking and steep climbs. At one point, I wondered if he had actually gotten lost, but I think that too was a component of the misdirection.

I can't blame him. The previous time I went fishing with him I caught an 18-inch brown trout and lost another at least as large. Today, he offered to show me a spot great for "holdover" trout—stocked fish that escape the opening day hordes and head downstream. Miles from the stocking truck, he said these fish swam until they came to deep, cold pools.

I had mentioned an interest in fly fishing, and Bill—who uses predominantly bait—graciously offered to watch while I fished, so as not to interrupt my experience. We got to a shady pool that looked a lot like the bigger creeks I used to fish in Pennsylvania. I watched the surface but could see no feeding activity, so I tied on my go-to fly, a pheasant tail nymph under an indicator.

I cast out and watched the orange indicator float through the pool. The surface exploded as a fish slammed into my indicator. I debated switching to a dry fly, but flipped my line back to the top of the hole, and immediately hooked a trout. I brought it in, and was surprised at the bright coloration of this rainbow trout. Rainbows don't reproduce in Iowa waters as the habitat is quite different than the fish's typical mountainous streams. This one still looked a far cry better than a recent hatchery release.

I handed the trout to Bill and cast again. Within seconds, I had another fish on. And so it went for the next hour. At one point, Bill suggested I try a bigger fly to catch the larger fish. I tied on a Clouser minnow, and began jerking it, and it reignited the pool. I hooked fish after fish. We kept a few for Bill to have for dinner and released the rest.

Bill had a family picnic to attend, so we left after a couple hours. I could have stayed, if I knew how to find my way out. The steep ravine hid any sign of humanity, or farming. I've fished far more famous waters that offered basically the same fishing scenario.

But Iowa still offered more. It was time to try for the state's wild, native brook trout.

━ ⌒ ━

Brook trout famously need cold, clean water and plenty of shade over said water. They historically ranged in streams around Eastern North America. They could be found in beaver ponds in Maine, along the coast in New England, in postcard-perfect streams meandering through hemlocks in Pennsylvania, and high in the Smoky Mountains.

Even in many of the East's famous trout streams, brook trout are gone, long ago replaced by a European introduction, brown trout. While brown trout can certainly compete with (and eat) brook trout, this is not simply a case of a non-native replacing the original inhabitant. The brown trout has a higher tolerance for warm water, lack of cover, and other habitat deficiencies. (Somewhat ironically, in the Western United States, where brook trout are not native, they have proliferated to plague proportions in many streams. The cold, mountain water suits them fine, and they're able to outcompete cutthroat trout and other native species.)

Iowa is the southwestern limit of the brook trout's range, and with the state's water quality issues and loss of natural habitat, it has not fared well. In fact, at one point no one was sure any native trout were left. There were rumors, but little else. The wild trout fisheries—the ones that could sustain themselves without stocking—consisted of brown trout. A non-native trout, yes, but one that could persist without constant assistance from hatcheries.

According to many reports, locals knew a small stream called South Pine Creek that still contained colorful brookies. This property was acquired in the 1990s by the Iowa Natural Heritage Foundation and became a state wildlife management area. And indeed, brookies swam the creek there. Genetic tests revealed this to be a unique strain closely related to fish in Minnesota.

"The hatchery brook trout we had were from East Coast populations," says Michael Siepker, an Iowa Department of Natural Resources (DNR) fisheries biologist. "Subsequent genetic tests have confirmed that."

That meant one known stream with wild, native fish—a treasure, but a fragile one. "Our work is to buffer against a catastrophic event on South Pine," says Siepker. "We had to identify other streams with the habitat conditions that could support and sustain wild brook trout populations."

Every year during the brook trout's spawning season, DNR biologists visit South Pine for electrofishing, running electric currents through the water that stuns but does not kill the fish. The biologists collect eggs from the native fish to rear in a hatchery. These genetically pure fish are then used to reintroduce brook trout into streams with suitable habitat.

To date, there are three streams in Iowa with solely wild brook trout and another nine that include wild brook trout as well as brown trout, but that are self-sustaining. These streams are not supplemented with hatchery stock.

Researchers are conducting further tests to see if the gene pool is sufficiently diverse. Three streams have also been stocked solely with a brook trout strain from nearby Wisconsin, and are similarly monitored.

A new effort has launched to see if there might be other relict brook trout populations still surviving in northeast Iowa. A graduate researcher, Brett Kelly, will spend his summers talking to landowners and electrofishing small streams in search of lost brookies.

"It's an interesting challenge," says Kelly. "Iowa DNR has fish tanks at the state fair, and I heard many people there saying they didn't know there were brook trout here. My job is to pinpoint waters that still have the conditions where brook trout could live, and then see what I find."

His goal is to survey two hundred streams over the next two years.

The reason all this work can occur is in no small part because many anglers want it done. The DNR has seen an increased interest in wild trout fishing through their trout angler survey, which seeks to understand what trout stamp purchasers (required for trout fishing) want from their experience. "There is no doubt that the interest in native trout is increasing," says Siepker. "I get a lot of inquiries. There are anglers who travel around and seek out native trout."

As with so many fisheries managers, balance comes into play. "There are anglers who want to go to a pond where it's stocked every day, and those who only want wild, native fish," he says. "You have people all along the spectrum. What constitutes a quality experience is defined differently. We have to offer a diversity of opportunities."

I had already had two quality experiences with Iowa trout fishing, both fun and successful, resulting in plenty of fish with family and friends. But to really see what quality trout fishing looked like here, I knew I wanted to catch the native fish. I had to go to South Pine.

I arrived at the wildlife management area parking lot early in the morning, dew still on the grass. The boundary of the area was sharply delineated; on the other side of the fence was, of course, a cornfield. I strung up my ultralight fly rod and followed a path down a hillside into woodlands.

The path hadn't been mowed, and it looked as if it hadn't been trod upon for some time. At first I felt glad to be fishing an unpressured stream, then wondered if I was in the wrong place. After twenty-five minutes of walking, that questioning only intensified, as I still hadn't found water.

A hen turkey strutted in a little forest opening, and I kicked up a doe with two fawns. Hardwoods stretched in front of me, with nary a sign of farming. A nice walk, but I wanted trout. The trail disappeared, and I found myself kicking through brush, stopping occasionally to pick ticks off my shirt. I finally came to a little meadow and saw flowing water. At first glance, I again harbored a suspicion that I had ended up in the wrong area. I stared at the deeply undercut bank, a sign of erosion and not exactly what I associated with brook trout.

I nonetheless stalked toward the edge . . . and saw two fish dart away. I scolded myself; brook trout can be skittish and I'd need a low profile and quiet approach. I got down on my hands and knees and crawled downstream. The water ran crystal clear, with a deep pool interspersed with little riffles. Trouty. I saw a splashy rise. I cast, and my fly caught on a weed, making the line land with an awkward thud. That fish, too, darted away.

I walked around a bend in the stream and could see a nice, deep hole ahead. I again crouched, stalking as if I was hunting rather than fishing. This time I landed a dry fly along the edge of the pool, and was rewarded with an immediate take. Despite the small size of the fish, it put a satisfying bend in my fiberglass rod. I pulled it to shore and gazed at the 6-inch fish: a grayish blue with yellow spots, and reddish fins and belly. It was the smallest trout I had caught on my Iowa fishing odyssey, but also the most beautiful.

I slipped the hook out of its mouth. I knew I wouldn't be able to put another fly through this small hole, as all the fish had scattered. I walked on, fishing each deep pool. Throughout the morning, trout would rise sporadically. I landed five more fish, and lost a couple others, each bright and spunky, each slamming my fly on the surface. A perfect morning.

I debated staying longer, but sometimes just a few fish is enough. I hiked out, the sun now high and humidity soaking through my quick-dry shirt. I drove through the rolling hills and stopped in Decorah, a small college town perhaps as surprising here as a native trout. I had a beer at Toppling Goliath Brewery, consistently rated by the hard-core beer nerds as one of the hottest craft beer producers in the country. My IPA was indeed hoppy and delicious, the perfect exclamation point to time on a trout stream. Another surprise.

Of course, no state is either its funny stereotype or its state tourism brochure. Even among the cornfields, there's more than meets the eye. During the course of researching this book, I've found that a fishing rod helps you find the beautiful and surprising places that still exist. But I find myself returning in my mind to those South Pine brook trout for other reasons. They're not just another native trout experience for the life list, and it's more than a novelty to catch trout in the land of corn.

With our global population approaching eight billion people, most land will not be pristine. A good portion of our planet is going to be allocated to producing food. And while there are ways to grow food that are better or worse for the environment, all of that agriculture will have some impact on wild things and freshwater.

If brook trout—fragile, finicky brook trout—can persist in the midst of some of the most heavily farmed country on Earth, maybe we can hold onto our wildlife after all. If we can restore and reintroduce native fish in Iowa, why not elsewhere? Those speckled, feisty fish, leaping at the fly, suggest possibility—the possibility for restoring native species, not just in the wild and remote places, but anywhere streams flow.

CHAPTER FIVE

Other Bass

Everything about the scene around me suggests smallmouth bass fishing. I'm in a driftboat on a small, riffle-filled river. I'm casting Clouser minnows hard against the banks and into little pools. The day falls into a familiar rhythm: cast, strip, strip, strip.

When the hits come, it *feels* like smallmouth fishing. Aggressive takes, strong runs. When I first glimpse the fish in the clear water, you guessed it: the fish *looks* like a smallmouth bass, too.

Then it's time for a closer look. This fish is more yellow, with prominent bars covering its body. There's a superficial resemblance to a smallmouth, but this is a more striking creature. It's the Texas state fish, the Guadalupe bass.

I'm in the Texas Hill Country with Nature Conservancy colleague and friend John Karges and fly-fishing guide Alvin Dedeaux for a day pursuing these fish.

Already I love them: attractive, hard-fighting, and found in scenic, largely unvisited rivers. They swim only in this region. However, Guadalupe bass face a significant threat to their existence. And that threat is, ironically enough, smallmouth bass.

❧

Fishing is as faddish as any other pastime. Not so long ago, largemouth and smallmouth bass were considered vastly inferior to trout, little more than "trash fish." In 1881, James A. Henshall published *The Book of the Black Bass* to persuade anglers that these fish were worth pursuing.

Gradually, both species gained popularity. Ray Scott began the Bass Anglers Sportsman Society (BASS) and a series of bass fishing tournaments. It created not just a new professional sport but also a billboard for fancy boats and gear. Today, BASS has five hundred thousand members and the largemouth bass is the most popular game fish on the continent. Smallmouth bass have similarly become a popular sport fish, often pursued on rivers and large streams by anglers casting spinning lures or flies.

I continue to be mystified by the appeal of following bass fishing on television; the excitement of watching paint dry comes to mind. I find the techniques of modern bassing—fast boats and heavy rods that essentially winch fish out of their lair—to be among the most boring in the sport. None of that should hide the fact that these are great game species. In their place.

The problem is—mirroring what happened with trout—the rise in popularity of bassing has meant the spread of bass around the country. Many anglers have come to appreciate the diversity of species and subspecies of native trout, and have worked to protect and restore them. Many of those same anglers are surprised to learn that there is also a diversity of native bass beyond largemouths and smallmouths.

The taxonomy of black bass, as these fish are known, is actually poorly understood. New genetic evidence reveals that there are more species of these fish than thought. The Southeast—in particular Georgia, Alabama, and Northern Florida—is home to native bass species that live in small, mountain streams much like trout.

Many of these bass species have been isolated in specific river basins, evolving into new subspecies and species. But just as biologists are unraveling the taxonomy, they're realizing they may be too late. Many of these fish have already hybridized with introduced bass species, some stocked by state agencies and some stocked by "bucket biologists."

Fisheries researchers are currently in agreement (generally) of nine species of black bass, but there could be more. The black bass include the perennial favorites like the largemouth and small-mouth bass, but also some pretty much unknown to the typical bass boat owner. Many states across the country are bass crazy, but that love is somewhat narrow.

Take Texas, a state that embraces the glitz of competitive largemouth bass fishing. Sparkling boats glide across reservoirs in search of trophy fish. This is a state that has a program called Share Lunker. It encourages anglers who have caught a trophy bass to keep it alive, and share it with the Texas Department of Parks and Wildlife. The agency breeds them in a quest to create "super bass," a genetic lineup of trophies to stock in state waterways.

As much as I enjoy fishing for largemouth bass (although I prefer casting a popper in a farm pond to sitting in a decked-out boat), the bass that drew me to Texas was the Guadalupe, a native, endemic species.

While it's the Texas state fish, the Guadalupe bass faces its own problems from non-native species. In the 1970s and 1980s, the Texas Parks and Wildlife Department stocked smallmouths, which quickly outcompeted and hybridized with Guadalupe bass. In some rivers, Guadalupe bass essentially disappeared. Researchers searching for the native fish in the Blanco River in the 1990s couldn't find a single pure specimen.

"It is embarrassing that we almost lost our state fish," says Rachael Ranft, The Nature Conservancy's North Hill Country project director. "In some waters, we probably will never be able to completely recover the Guadalupe bass population. But there have been a couple of promising methods in restoring them."

The Texas Parks and Wildlife Department began an ambitious stocking program, with the goal of releasing so many Guadalupe bass fingerlings into a creek that they essentially swamped the smallmouth bass population.

Biologists focused on Johnson Creek, a system that still had some Guadalupe bass, and had a dam in the tailwaters that prevented smallmouth migration upstream from the Guadalupe River. The stocking worked, and after several years Guadalupe bass accounted for 98 percent of the population.

"They are able to achieve this with continuous stocking," says Ranft. "When they stopped stocking, the smallmouth bass came back. They are not able to leave that system alone."

Other rivers, like the Blanco, had not been a priority for repatriation because no Guadalupe bass remained. Oddly enough, native fish restoration in the Blanco soon received a big boost from the most unlikely of sources, a devastating drought.

The 2011 Texas drought made national news as it led to increased wildfires, poor range conditions, and drying rivers. Drying rivers are generally not considered a boon to fish conservation. But in this case, they may have changed the future for Guadalupe bass in the Blanco River. The river's halfway point is called "The Narrows," a section of river that is a pinch point with steep bluffs on each side and a series of waterfalls, creating a barrier to fish passage except during flooding.

During the drought, the Upper Blanco above the falls severely dried up, with a series of disconnected pools constituting the only remaining water. This concentrated nearly every fish in the upper river. Biologists saw an opportunity.

They electroshocked and seined each pool, removing all smallmouth bass and other non-native fish. Due to the natural fish barrier, they were able to remove invasive species from a large stretch of river.

In April 2012, heavy rains had the river flowing again. Biologists stocked approximately 105,000 Guadalupe bass, followed by 122,000 more in 2013. They also stocked the river below The Narrows with Guadalupes, even though smallmouths couldn't effectively be removed there.

A river survey in 2014 revealed that the upper river had a 100 percent pure Guadalupe bass population; the lower river was 50 percent Guadalupes, and stocked fish were already reproducing successfully.

Then came a catastrophic 2015 flood that created temporary fish passage over the waterfalls. "But even that flood brought really good news," says Ranft. "The upper river was still 100 percent Guadalupes, and about 55 percent pure below the falls."

This spring Ranft joined the Texas Parks and Wildlife Department in additional stocking of the river, with 55,794 fingerlings released.

"The goal is to someday not have to stock the river at all, to have a self-sustaining population," she says. "The downstream population may never be entirely Guadalupe bass, but the upper river could potentially have a thriving population of native fish that would potentially supply the lower half of the river."

And this restoration could also be replicated on other rivers. In some waters, Guadalupe bass face additional issues, like dams. They fare better in flowing waters with lots of riffles, so dammed water is not ideal habitat. "We're working to find solutions for landowners so they can get the same benefits of dams while restoring fish habitat," she says.

While there are some anglers who would still rather fish for smallmouths, Ranft believes most she encounters now recognize the uniqueness of the Guadalupe bass fishery. "They've been very supportive," she says. "This is a special fish, found only here. More and more anglers see that as very appealing."

❦

I let my fly sink a few seconds and began stripping line. The fly moved a few feet and stopped, just as it had for the past four casts. I lifted my rod and was tight on a spunky fish.

My rod bent and I continued pulling line, bringing in a nice white bass. I admired the fish and released it. "How many is that now?" a voice asked behind me.

I swiveled around and saw John Karges sitting on a bank above me. I hadn't noticed he was there. "I saw you catch those last five," he said. "You must be over twenty fish by now."

"Yeah, it's more than twenty," I replied.

Karges, with his white beard, weathered face and tanned arms, looks like he just stepped out of a nature documentary. This effect is heightened by his preference for khaki outdoor clothes. And that initial assessment holds: Karges is a walking encyclopedia on reptiles, birds, paleontology, folklore, and native plants.

I'd long heard about Karges's field skills from colleagues at the Nature Conservancy. Karges is associate director of field science for the Conservancy's Texas Chapter; he also is an active science communicator, running a couple of popular Facebook interest groups on natural history and conservation. My colleagues praised his enthusiasm, his scientific integrity, and his storytelling, but what I noticed is they always mentioned one thing: "You never met someone who loves to fish so much."

Karges had suggested this spot on the Pedernales River for our first day. While he expressed doubts about the quality of the fishing, pretty much as soon as we started casting in the Hill Country River, we began having bass hit our streamers.

Just before lunch, I even caught a couple fish bearing a superficial resemblance to smallmouth bass, except with bright barring on their sides. Both were small, but undeniably Guadalupe bass.

By late afternoon, Karges and I had caught nearly seventy fish between us, and we decided to hit a barbeque restaurant and get a good night's rest. Tomorrow, he had planned a guided float trip specifically for Guadalupe bass.

I admit a certain ambivalence about fishing guides. I've had some great ones, guides that have been like fishing with old friends. As anyone who has stepped into a fly shop along a big-name river like the Henry's Fork knows, though, the field has become dominated by too-cool brahs who are livin' the dream by shouting orders at the idiots who pay them.

The next morning, it quickly became apparent that Alvin Dedeaux did not fit this model. One of the few African American fly-fishing guides I've met, his dreadlocks would reach nearly to his shins if he didn't tie them up in a huge roll over his head. Laid back, he's not one to shout orders or constantly nag on casting style. He just wants to fish.

As he readied his boat, he asked how our day on the Pedernales had been. "We each caught more than thirty fish," Karges said.

"That's not what a guide wants to hear," Dedeaux said with a laugh. "We aren't catching thirty fish today. We might catch some nice ones, if we're lucky. But not thirty fish."

Another fly-fishing guide, a friend and colleague of Dedeaux's, pulled in beside us with another client. "This will probably be the only fisherman we see today," says Dedeaux. "I think we'll have the river to ourselves."

That was in part due to lack of interest in Guadalupe bass and in part because of Texas's lack of public property. There were few access points on this river, and the occasionally shallow water favored smaller drift boats over big, shiny gas guzzlers.

We were fishing the Colorado River, a medium-sized river not to be confused with the famous one that flows through the Grand Canyon. This one flows into the Gulf of Mexico. It was never stocked with smallmouth bass, so the Guadalupe bass have persisted without hybridization. Fishing here was what fishing in the Texas Hill Country should be. Fat, feisty, native bass.

We motored up river, past herons on logs, cattle grazing along the stream, and patches of forest. Then Dedeaux cut the motor and took to the oars. We began drifting back down the river. I had on a Clouser minnow similar to yesterday; Karges had a sinking leech to plumb deeper depths.

"We need to find out where they are," Dedeaux said. "We may be changing flies a bit."

We cast close to the bank, and Dedeaux told us to pay special attention to riffles and pools alongside riffles. We again fell into the rhythm of anglers. Cast, strip, strip, strip.

Nothing.

The other driftboat came floating by, the client throwing graceful loops. "Anything?" Dedeaux called out.

Both the client and guide shrugged. "Nothing. Not a bump."

"That guy fishes all the time," said Dedeaux. "Great caster. Fishes a lot for steelhead and bonefish. So at least we know it's not something we're doing wrong. The fish just aren't biting."

After an hour, casting a streamer becomes almost trancelike, what some mindfulness experts now call "flow." Cast, strip, strip, strip, strip, BAM! And there it was. Or was it?

I felt a definite tug, but so quick that I questioned whether it actually was a bass.

"Bump?" Dedeaux asked.

"Maybe," I said.

Ten minutes later, there was no doubt. The fish swirled out of a back-eddy, slamming the Clouser almost as soon as it hit the water. I set the hook. And missed.

"At least we know it won't be impossible," Dedeaux said. He kept rowing.

Soon thereafter, another strike, and another miss. In my head, I began the angler's version of self talk, part chastising and part pep rally.

The other boat had pulled off on a sandbar, with the guide and client making sandwiches. We pulled in alongside and joined them for a shore lunch. The well-traveled client raised his eyes at us. "Slow day?"

"I had two strikes but missed both," I said.

"As I always say, it's better to have hooked and lost than to never have hooked at all," the client said, in what was to be a recurring theme in my travels. Fishing clichés. They really aren't just on bumper stickers. Anglers say them all the time.

The client then began telling of his upcoming trips, to British Columbia, the Bahamas, the Florida Keys. As interesting as this was, Karges and I were eager to get back on the river. I had some missed strikes to atone for.

Dedeaux pushed off and we drifted past a herd of cows, then back through quiet woods with no signs of people. Only a few minutes into the drift, a bass hammered my fly. And once again, I missed. Then Karges had a strike. He, too, missed.

"Do the strip set, fellows," Dedeaux said. "Keep stripping that line hard when they strike. Then raise the rod."

Now I was all focus. I glanced at Karges and saw determination in his eyes. I cast into a riffle and began stripping, and saw a shadow dart out of overhanging roots. This time I set the hook—into what was the smallest bass so far.

But still a Guadalupe. I stripped line in and brought the fish to the side of the boat. I had a beautiful if little native bass. There's nothing like a fish in the boat to renew hope. At least we wouldn't be skunked.

The fishing, if not exactly hot, turned on enough so that we could expect a strike every few minutes. Karges was next, catching a large and beautiful Guadalupe. Soon thereafter he hooked a nice largemouth that rocketed out of the water in a boiling splash.

I cast into a pool and had a fish dart out, swipe, and miss my lure. I cast again and this time, it smashed the Clouser, as if in rage at having let its prey get away the last time. I brought the nice fish to the boat.

We kept drifting, and casting, and catching. Almost all the fish were Guadalupes. Beautiful native fish. Still here.

Of course, any river is only one ill-informed angler with a bucket away from an invasive species, as I had already found in Yellowstone and other waters. Such a thoughtless action could change the ecosystem, the course of native fish conservation, and the fishing prospects.

While attitudes have changed toward Guadalupe bass, keeping them in rivers would require constant vigilance and support from anglers.

On the Colorado, as the day wore on, the bites slowed and we approached the takeout. "Give it a few more casts. Let's get one more," Dedeaux said.

The next cast my fly hit a small whirlpool and—wham!—a nice fish slammed my fly. My rod bent deeply, and a few minutes later we had a bass in the net.

"Perfect," Dedeaux said, the sun setting over the river.

Karges and I smiled. There was nothing more to say.

I released the bass, grateful to encounter another native species with my fly rod. Long may the Guadalupe bass swim the Hill Country, and may they reclaim their home rivers from our fishy mistakes.

CHAPTER SIX

Big Gonads and Sneaker Males

My Rapala hit next to the lily pads, and I began a slow retrieve. It had been a slow night, but any minute that would change. It always did.

I drove out to this little lake nearly every night, casting shiners in deep water and working lures in places I knew bass lurked. As the sun set, I'd tie on a black Jitterbug and pitch it out, listening to the plug churn along the surface, waiting for the explosive top-water strike of a largemouth. Often, I'd miss the hook set. But I still caught plenty of fish.

A day after I graduated from Penn State, I started working as a writer for the university's performing arts center. I interviewed performers for feature stories and edited the programs that concertgoers would receive. My daily life suddenly became a steady churn of deadlines. I took to the water to destress, a recurring pattern in my life.

Stone Valley Lake was a short distance away. I first visited it in high school as part of a program called Conservation Leadership School. I had little time to fish, but one free evening I left my classmates around the fire and crept along the lake for a few minutes. In five casts, I caught two bass, a feat unheard of at this point in my life. I resolved to return.

The region around the university is justifiably famous for its trout fishing, so most weeknight evenings I had Stone Valley to myself.

Then one slow night, the sounds of a rumbling engine drew my attention from the water. A battered old Ford Bronco stopped and a large, disheveled man spilled out. He looked to be in his sixties, but I surmised that hard living might have added a few years. His shirt was hopelessly wrinkled and a bit soiled; his white hair was uncombed. He made audible grunts as he pulled rod and tackle box from his vehicle. He staggered. I wondered if he was drunk.

He careened down the hill and set up about 30 yards away. I felt mildly annoyed by the intrusion. The man spent about fifteen minutes tying his line, baiting his hook and attaching a gigantic red-and-white bobber. Finally, he wound back, let out a pig-like grunt and let his line fly. It went maybe 6 feet. He mumbled something, brought it back in and repeated the process.

I began catching fish, and I could feel him staring at me. And then I heard a yell. "Whoa!" he roared, as he pulled back on his rod as if setting the hook on a marlin. I saw the glimpse of a tiny bluegill, but it slipped off the hook. He repeated this process, over and over. He appraised me as if preparing to make conversation, and I decided to leave.

I returned the next night, and this man was already there. He waved to me as I got out of the car. I set up farther away, but within twenty minutes he had moved closer. The next evening: there he was again. This time, he called as soon as I got out of the car, his voice slurring. "Hey, I could use help with these bluegills."

Help with bluegills? Help with the simplest of fish, the one that most of us learned to catch as little kids? Don't we know all there is to know about bluegills by the time we're age twelve?

It turns out, I was completely wrong about this man. It turns out that I also was completely wrong about bluegills.

—◦—

Consider the bluegill: ubiquitous, tasty, and easy to catch. It's the first fish many anglers land. You don't need fancy gear; cheap Spiderman and Barbie rods from Walmart have caught untold thousands of bluegills. So have strings tied to sticks.

Fishing is often promoted as one of the ideal opportunities to introduce kids to the outdoors. There's one major flaw in this: most forms of fishing demand patience. While my three-year-old son has many virtues, I can assure you patience is not one of them. If you want to "hook a kid on fishing," you do not go on a steelhead trip, standing in the rain for days on end, convinced against all evidence that the next cast will hook a fish (come to think of it, this is not all that much fun for me, either).

But I can go to the local playground and let my son play on the slides and swings while I get his little Dock Demon rod ready. He can wander over and we can cast together. Within a minute, the bobber will be dancing around. Very little patience required. You can make a fifteen-minute bluegill expedition and realistically catch fish.

After he's had his fill, I'll sometimes pull out my two-weight fiberglass fly rod and cast out little nymphs, catching fish after fish after fish. The aggressive bluegills put a satisfying bend in the light rod. Maybe it's nostalgia, maybe it's because sometimes you just need easy fish, but the bluegill doesn't get old. Many anglers young and old still love them.

Familiarity may not lead to contempt, but it can lead to a false sense of knowledge. Many anglers have caught an awful lot of bluegills, so there are a lot of bluegill experts out there. Contrary to popular belief, catching hundreds or even thousands of fish is not scientific research.

One thing everyone knows about bluegills is they're prone to stunting. On some lakes, you will catch 5- and 6-inch fish all day long, but never one of the 9-inchers that make for a satisfying meal. Anglers have long declared this was due to fish overpopulation; if you don't kill enough bluegills, they quickly take over the lake and become stunted runts.

It's why bluegill limits are generous in many states, allowing anglers to keep twenty-five or more per day. You really can't kill too many, conventional wisdom suggests. I once went fishing at a large pond with a high school friend, and he pitched every bluegill into the field. When I questioned why he was killing them if he didn't want to eat them, he replied, "We have to do this, or we'll never catch a nice one out of this pond. It's for the good of the fish."

The fish gasping in the summer air would likely disagree. But random cruelty aside, the general management program does appeal to common sense. An overpopulated population is not a healthy population.

A lot of bluegill management is based on this common sense. But common sense is not the same as science, either.

⚬⚬⚬

I first met Andrew Rypel at a happy hour on a warm summer evening, as graduate students enjoyed craft beers overlooking Lake Mendota on the University of Wisconsin campus in Madison. I was meeting with doctoral candidates and postdocs connected to the University of Wisconsin's Department of Limnology, to my mind one of the finest centers for freshwater research in the world.

I was on a road trip seeking fish conservation stories, and I had just discussed a research project involving mahseer, undoubtedly one of the world's coolest game fishes. As my mind drifted toward the absolutely necessary trip to Thailand to cover this story, Rypel brought my head out of the clouds and into the lake right in front of me.

"I'm doing some interesting work on bluegills," he said. "There's a lot more going on with them than many anglers realize."

The happy hour was winding down, so we decided to discuss more over a little fishing on Lake Mendoka the next evening. Less than twenty-four hours later I met Rypel, then a fisheries biologist with the Wisconsin DNR, and postdoctoral fisheries student Pete Lisi at the little pier adjoining the Department of Limnology's lab.

Appropriately enough for a bluegill discussion, Rypel brought a couple containers full of nightcrawlers. We rigged up lines with bobbers, cast out and caught fish all evening: yellow perch, small-mouth bass, and, yes, plenty of bluegills.

"With panfish, you have a really diverse pool of anglers," said Rypel. "It isn't a type of fishing that is just for specialists. You have beginning anglers. You have casual anglers. They're the fish for everyone."

Rypel grew up catching plenty of bluegills with his family. "We would go out and catch one hundred fish between us," he said. "We would fill the freezer. With bluegills, there's still a fill-the-freezer mentality with many anglers. It's one of the last bastions for that mentality."

Based on conventional wisdom, this heavy harvest should result in plenty of large bluegills. After all, bluegills need to be harvested so they don't become stunted. But instead, anglers notice that it's becoming harder and harder to find nice fish.

"Avid anglers know they're catching fewer big bluegills. Their solution is to try to harvest their way out of the problem," said Rypel. "The research we're doing shows that on many lakes, it's not under-harvest that's leading to smaller bluegills. It's the exact opposite. We're keeping too many."

Rypel had heard the complaints of anglers, but he also noticed that savvy anglers looking for big bluegills tended to go off the beaten path, to lakes that were difficult to reach. They intuitively visited lakes where harvest was lighter, not the ones where people kept every bluegill they caught.

He conducted an analysis of Wisconsin fishing records and found that bluegill size has steadily decreased over a thirty-year period. When harvest regulations were loosened—such as when the panfish bag limit increased after soldiers returned from World War II—bluegill sizes showed rapid size reductions.

In response to the trend, the Wisconsin DNR reduced the bag limit from twenty-five fish to ten fish on ten lakes as a test. Researchers, including Rypel, analyzed fish size before and after the regulation. They found that fish size increased on average a half inch on maximum size and more than three-quarters of an inch on mean size. For a fish that is 6–10 inches, that's a significant increase.

When Rypel and I talked on that summer dock, he thought the size decrease might be due to an interesting facet of bluegill natural history: namely, big gonads. In the spring, large bluegill males set up territories; the bigger and more aggressive the male, the better the location of the spawning bed. At the center of the colony, in the best position to fend off predators and other males, is the top contender.

"These males put all their energy into defending the nest and competing with the other male bluegills for the best females," said Rypel. "All their energy goes into body growth. Being a parental male is a tough business, but his first goal is to attract a fantastic female mate. The female leaves after laying eggs, and the male has to guard the nest."

But here's the wild card: Not all males participate in the festivities. As the jocks of the bluegill realm fight over the prime spots, the small nerds hide around the edges, waiting for their chance.

"Bluegill males can have two completely different life histories," said Rypel. "Some males opt out completely from growing big and guarding spawning beds. They become what we call sneaker males."

Sneaker males are small. They do not look like they could win any battle. To an untrained eye, they may look like a different species.

Whereas the parental male puts all his energy into a big, strong body, the sneaker male puts all the energy into giant gonads. "The sneaker male has stunted growth, but his testes are blown up like balloons," says Rypel. "Whatever energy he acquires goes right into the testes."

While the parental males are battling and protecting the spawning bed, the sneaker males are roving around. And when the parental males are courting females, or fighting, the sneaker males, true to their name, sneak right onto the spawning bed.

"Because they have these huge testes, they have a lot of sperm," says Rypel.

The parental males on their spawning beds are highly aggressive and visible. This makes them a popular target among anglers. Drop a jig on a spawning bed and the big parental male will attack it. Meanwhile, the sneaker males remain out of view of humans.

When we fished on that fine Wisconsin evening, Rypel hypothesized that anglers targeting the big, parental males removed the fish with the best genetics (and those with the largest size) from the population, leaving the breeding entirely to sneaker males. But he was just starting his research, so he couldn't say for sure. Even with common fish, questions can't be answered without the scientific process.

More than two years later, I gave Rypel (now the Peter B. Moyle and California Trout Chair with the University of California, Davis) a call to see how the research had progressed. When I asked about the sneaker males, he laughed.

"With the sneakers, it was the exact opposite of what I thought it would be," he said. "That's why you have to do the research."

Rypel sampled bluegills in twenty-three lakes, ranging from those with very low or no harvest rates to those that were absolutely pounded by anglers. "It was very hard to find the lakes with low exploitation," he said. "We had to go to some preserves that didn't allow fishing."

In these low-exploitation lakes, he found the full-size range of bluegills, including plenty of 8- and 9-inch fish. "Some of those fish were thirteen years old," he said.

About 20 percent of the male bluegills in these lakes were sneaker males. When he checked the highly fished lakes, he found very few large fish. "In some lakes, it's hard to find anything over 6 inches," he said.

The big surprise for him was these pressured lakes also contained very few sneaker males. Only 0–5 percent of the males exhibited this trait. Sneaker males were not proliferating in over-fished lakes after all.

Rypel now offered another hypothesis. In a lake with little harvest, and lots of big males, the little ones have to use anything they can to have an advantage. This results in many adopting the sneaker male lifestyle.

In a lake where all the big fish have been removed, this makes being a sneaker male a much less effective mating strategy. When all the fish are small, almost any male can realistically guard his own spawning bed. There's very little chance of being run off by a 9-inch bruiser.

Rypel also believes that a lake full of small males might have led to the idea of stunted bluegills. Imagine fishing a lake full of spawning beds, all occupied by junior-sized specimens, whereas ten years ago there were fewer but bigger bluegills. That might look like an over-populated lake.

The next phase of research in Wisconsin involves placing a hundred lakes under more restrictive management. A third of those lakes will have a ten-bluegill limit, a third will have a five-bluegill limit, and a third will have a five-bluegill limit only during the spawning season, with the rest of the year retaining the usual limit of twenty-five bluegills.

These experimental regulations will be in place for a minimum of ten years, offering an excellent look at how more conservative harvest affects bluegills. As Rypel notes, it still allows plenty of lakes in Wisconsin for a family to catch large limits of panfish.

While many anglers know that bluegill size has decreased, some still challenge the research. It's true that different lakes may require different management regimes. In small ponds, predators like largemouth bass may play a greater role in regulating bluegill size. But for quality fishing to continue, anglers may have to accept a bit of regulatory complexity. Rypel acknowledges that having different regulations on different lakes can create challenges for anglers, especially for new or casual participants.

"It can be tough for kids to know what the rules are, there's no doubt about it," he said. "But regulation complexity does allow for greater creativity. It allows us to do better research that benefits the fishery, and that ultimately benefits the angler."

I think of those old, black-and-white photos of fishermen in national parks, proudly hoisting stringers holding fifty cutthroat trout. Today, we look at that and see unnecessary excess. We accept that we just can't go to the local stream and catch dozens of trout, at least not if we want to have any good fishing left next year.

I suspect we'll reach that point with bluegills and other species, too. When Rypel expanded his focus to look at the trends of other Wisconsin game fish, he found interesting results. Five species— largemouth bass, smallmouth bass, lake sturgeon, northern pike, and sauger—remained fairly stable in size. Muskellunge dropped initially but then rebounded. Interestingly, all of these species are heavily managed and a strong catch-and-release ethic has become the norm. By contrast, panfish species declined in size. Bluegills are only one species of sunfish, and many others receive even less management attention. Ensuring the future of fishing ultimately will require that all species are managed. It will require a cultural shift from anglers, but ultimately it will benefit the sport.

━◦～

I didn't think about bluegill management back in those days on Stone Valley Lake. I didn't think about much except catching the next bass. But I responded when the disheveled man asked me for help with bluegills.

He introduced himself as Tom Montgomery. I looked at his fishing rig and immediately could offer some tips. His hook was several sizes too big, for starters. "Use a smaller hook, and wait until the bobber goes under," I said. "And you don't have to set the hook so hard."

He chuckled and thanked me. "It's been a while since I've done this, still figuring it all out," he said. His speech slightly slurred, but I detected no alcohol.

The next evening, he again waved me over. He had on a smaller hook. He mentioned that he had caught a couple of sunfish so far. A loon called out on the lake. "That kind of reminds me of Thoreau," he said. "Have you ever read him? He has good ideas, but not enough fishing."

I suspected that whatever story I had written about this man in my head was wrong. I began asking him that most banal of questions, what he did for work. "Oh, I'm retired now," he said. "Before that, nothing very interesting."

That turned out to be not quite true, as I'd find out over the weeks and months ahead. Tom had been a PhD geologist, working for an engineering firm. He moved up the ranks. He published papers. He worked all the time. This is, of course, not an unusual story.

One day during this workaholic binge he took stock of his life. He felt alienated from his wife. His daughters wanted nothing to do with him. He had no hobbies, no interests, outside of work. "I realized I had put all my eggs in one basket," he said. "I fished as a kid. I thought maybe it would be time to pick that up again."

He bought a fishing magazine, but that's as far as it got. He worked as much as ever, with no time for anything else. Six months later, he wrecked his truck into a telephone pole, totaling the vehicle and himself. Emergency workers pried him out, and he had suffered many broken bones and a bashed-in head. He emerged from the hospital dizzy, unable to concentrate. Speaking took effort. He thought it would pass. It didn't.

"It was time to go fishing," he said the first time he told me.

"I'm sorry," I said.

He shrugged. "It was time to go fishing," he repeated.

Then he whipped one of his excessive casts into the pond. He became more proficient at catching bluegills. He usually caught a few during the evenings. I'd assist in getting them off the hook. He'd come over to admire my bass and pickerel. One night, I saw a smile on his face as he reeled in another fish, and I had the obvious thought that Tom Montgomery was a bit of a fishing cliché. I'm pretty sure a song based on his life would top the modern country charts. But the bumper stickers and social media memes about spending too much time at the office resonate for a reason. Fishing is an antidote to the stressful life, in no small part because it comes with memories of simpler times. For Tom, when he began to question his single-minded devotion to his work, his thoughts turned to ponds and bobbers and bluegills.

Of course, embedded in nostalgia is the idea that life was simpler and things were better way back when. That may be a harmless enough belief, but it doesn't mean that bluegills should be managed like they were in the "good old days." There are anglers who believe that more regulations ruin the simple experience of fishing, but is that really true?

My friend Tom almost never kept a fish. Lowering the bag limit to ten bluegills, or to five, would not have mattered. The solace fishing brought him did not correlate to a heavy stringer. I've yet to see a bumper sticker that says *A bad day of fishing is better than a good day of work, but only if you fill your freezer.*

Like so much in our world, even something as simple as a little fish on the end of your line is so easy to misunderstand, to get completely wrong. It's good for fishing to remain at least partly in the realm of mystery. But fishing management does not have that luxury—not if fishing is going to survive as a viable activity in the 21st century.

CHAPTER SEVEN

Cisco Disco

They stand like sentinels, lining the shoreline, long-handled nets at the ready. Camouflage is the uniform of the day, although some wear snowmobile suits or puffy NFL jackets. Their faces stare into the water, as if willing fish to appear, or the cold to dissipate. It's 25 degrees Fahrenheit and windy. Waves lap at waders.

I'm here for the Cisco Disco, an annual event on the Utah portion of Bear Lake. Enthusiasts line up to net their limit of Bonneville cisco, a species of fish found only here. The cisco resembles a freshwater sardine, although it's actually a white-fish and in the same family as salmon and trout. Approximately 7.5 million cisco live in Bear Lake, and in mid-January many of them come close to shore to spawn. And people show up to catch and eat them.

The Cisco Disco is timed to coincide with the cisco spawning run, but it's unpredictable and appears to be getting later each year. No one seems all that concerned. A festive atmosphere prevails, with families grilling sausages, drinking hot chocolate, telling stories of previous discos. A few trade their nets for spinning rods, hoping to entice one of the lake's trophy cutthroat. They don't seem to be having luck, either, and I see several chipping ice out of the rod guides.

The wind continues to roil the surface, reducing water clarity. Based on what I've learned about cisco, it seems unlikely they'll show today.

I make my way back to my car and meet two college students, Steve Baran and Zach Hoopes, on a weekend outing from Weber State University. They're joking and periodically scanning the shores for any sign of activity.

"Hunting season's over, the homework's done, we thought it would be something fun to do on a winter day," says Hoopes.

"We just love different outdoor adventures," Baran tells me.

"We have nowhere else to be," says Hoopes. "If we weren't here, we'd be sitting at home by the fire, probably watching Netflix."

"I'm not going to lie, you make that sound pretty good right now," Baran says with a laugh.

The fish never do make an appearance. But everyone here knows it's only a matter of time. Maybe tomorrow, maybe next week. They'll come.

At Bear Lake, unlike so many other lakes plagued by invasive species and pollution and a host of other issues, the native fish species still abound. They annually show up in the shallows, where hardy anglers can appreciate them in all their glory.

Why did Bear Lake escape the fate of so many other waters? In a word: luck. A lot of the mistakes that characterized early fisheries management somehow didn't take hold here. And today, scientific management is working, keeping native fish abundant and anglers happy. If you're looking for a model of what the future of freshwater fishing could be, you would do well to start at Bear Lake.

Bear Lake occupies more than 100 square miles, straddling the southeast corner of Idaho and the northeast corner of Utah. A lot of tourist brochures and travel editorials dub it the "Caribbean of the Rockies" for its aqua-blue water. Visit in the summer, and you'll see throngs of visitors picnicking at state parks lining the lake's banks, or boating, kayaking, jet skiing, and paddleboarding in the lake. Buses of tourists, on package holidays to western national parks, make a stop here between Salt Lake City and Yellowstone.

The area has an old-fashioned family vacation vibe, with small stores hawking burgers and milkshakes, and plenty of places to buy or rent recreational equipment.

One thing you won't see much of in the summer, though, is people fishing. Or at least, fishing successfully.

"Oddly, the summer months are the absolute worst time to fish on Bear Lake," says Scott Tolentino, Bear Lake fisheries biologist for the Utah Division of Wildlife Resources.

That's because Bear Lake's fish population is one of the most unique in the world. Four of the fish are endemic species, found nowhere else. "Usually you mention endemic species in a freshwater lake, and you can safely assume they're endangered species," says Tolentino. "Here, none of the four are endangered. Three are sport fish, and anglers can catch and keep them."

These species—the Bonneville whitefish, Bear Lake whitefish, Bonneville cisco, and Bear Lake sculpin—tend to live in the deep waters in the middle of Bear Lake. But they come to the rocky shore to spawn. They've evolved so that each arrives at a different time, beginning with the Bonneville whitefish in late November.

A unique strain of cutthroat trout also lives in the lake, as well as other native fish like the Utah sucker and Utah chub. Sterile lake trout are stocked for sport fishing, but the lake lacks many of the problems associated with invasive species that plague so many lakes across North America. But that's not for lack of trying.

"In early fisheries management attempts, both Utah and Idaho tried stocking many different exotic species without regard to how they would affect the endemic species, but none of them were successful," says Tolentino. "It was just what fisheries managers did back then. They stocked lakes believing they'd improve them."

Fisheries managers stocked bluegills, kokanee, largemouth bass, rainbow trout, and other species. While some non-native species exist in the lake, none have prospered. The unique habitat conditions have proved unsuitable. Even the adaptable carp, found in rivers that connect to the lake, have failed to establish themselves here.

"Are there carp in Bear Lake? Yes. Can they spawn? No," says Tolentino. "You see a carp in here and it will look emaciated. This lake is a carp's hell hole. Once they get into the lake from the Bear River, they spend the rest of their lives trying to get out."

The native cutthroat trout are perhaps the luckiest of all. Managers stocked a variety of different subspecies, but later genetic tests revealed that today's cutthroat trout have remained genetically distinct. These fish were hit hard by early overfishing, but a hatchery program stocks cutthroat with the native genetics to supplement the wild population.

In so many places I traveled, I would be left imagining what the place would have been like before people mucked it up. Bear Lake is not a time capsule from the 1700s. But I could still experience the fishery in its glory. With four endemic species, each coming to shallow water at different times of year, my biggest question was: What species do I try for first?

I marked the Cisco Disco on my calendar, but I first had a chance to fish the Bonneville whitefish run a month earlier. I've long been a fan of mountain whitefish, an unfairly maligned denizen of Western trout streams. These fish typically eat insects and other small aquatic invertebrates, and I enjoy drifting nymphs through riffles to catch them.

A Bonneville whitefish is like your standard mountain whitefish that's had way too much Red Bull. When it reaches about 13 inches, its diet is almost exclusively other fish. They're extremely aggressive, and Tolentino has found whitefish with a dozen sculpin in their guts.

In December, these whitefish spawn in the rocky shallows and aggressively strike jigs and spinners. How could I resist?

Even before my first cast, though, my trip started to fall apart. A blizzard was heading toward the area, threatening to strand me.

I had a meeting with my new boss in two days, and couldn't afford to be sitting in a snowdrift. And so, what began as a full weekend of fishing suddenly had to be condensed into a couple of hours. This, too, is a reality of fishing in the 21st century.

After a four-hour drive, I dropped my wife and young son off at Lava Hot Springs in southeast Idaho. They could enjoy an afternoon of soaking while I drove another ninety minutes to fish. I promised I'd be back for my birthday party and the Big 10 championship game that evening.

I drove toward Garden City, Utah, the snow already beginning to accumulate on the roads. Trees danced in the wind, hardly the calm weather I hoped for. I arrived to find a different Bear Lake than the summer tourist scene. Most restaurants sported closed signs, and the small towns along the lake looked abandoned. While the Bonneville whitefish run is one of the big fishing events of the year, the remote locale and bitter weather conspired to keep fair-weather fishers away.

I pulled up to the Bear Lake Marina, with two jetties jutting out into the lake. A few boats with trailers were parked in the lot, and a couple more out on the jetty. As I got out of my car, an older man with two boys climbed up the jetty's rocks. The temperature hovered in the teens, with the wind whipping the lake into a froth. The boys wore only sweatshirts, and their faces and hands achieved the redness of boiled lobsters.

The man looked at me as I stepped out of the car. "We caught a cutthroat but no whitefish," he said. "And we were here two hours. I'd come back another time. Today's not the day."

Of course, if you fish much, you realize that today is almost never the day. I didn't have much choice anyhow. The man shrugged as I rigged up.

A short, impish man dressed in duck-hunting garb waved as I made my way down the jetty's slippery rocks to the lake. As I got my footing, he made his way over. The choppy lake's waves splattered my waders.

"Been having much luck this year?" the man asked.

"This is my first time fishing here," I said.

"Welcome!" he exclaimed. "Here's what you're gonna do. Tie on a jig, or a spinner. Put on a chunk of worm. Cast out as far as you can, and then count to ten to let it sink. Then reel it in sloooowly so that you are just off the bottom, just enough so you don't get snagged. That'll work. But today isn't the best day."

I followed his directions, slowly reeling my jig. And halfway to shore, I got snagged. I broke off the jig and tried again. Two casts later, my jig got stuck again. And so began a pattern of casting and losing lures.

My advisor left, and another family showed up and began fishing. I kept casting. I eventually figured out how not to hook one of the many rocks ringing the lake. That didn't help me catch fish. The family lasted about twenty minutes. I kept casting.

A few other groups came and went, and I didn't see anyone catch anything. A boat trolled about 100 yards offshore, and I did see a rod buckle once with a whitefish. This filled me with both hope and despair: at least the whitefish were around, but I wasn't able to cast that far.

I looked at my watch. I had already spent more than an hour here. Time was ticking. I hate fishing in a rush, but I decided to focus and make every cast count. I tied on a small Mepps spinner and tried something different. I just retrieved it steadily, not letting it sink to the bottom. A large cutthroat trout flashed the lure. Real hope now. I continued casting and steadily retrieving, but nothing else showed.

I moved about 30 yards to the point of the jetty. Ice coated my waders, coat, and rod. I looked at my watch: fifteen minutes left.

I walked a few yards and cast again. Bump. I set the hook and my ultralight wriggled. Fish on. It peeled line as I lifted the rod. I pumped and reeled, and the fish thrashed. With this fight, it had to be a nice cutthroat.

But as I got the fish closer to shore, I saw a sleek silvery shape. My first Bonneville whitefish. I hoisted the fish, slipped the spinner out of its mouth, and admired it for a second. It was about 14 inches, and as silvery as it appeared in the water. A beautiful fish, a prize that few anglers would ever catch.

I slipped it back into the lake. Fueled by the catch, I told myself I could make a few more casts—always a few more casts—but I caught nothing. My wader soles now frozen, it took me several minutes to make my way up the icy rocks. I blasted the car heater. It had been a short outing but I had encountered a new fish. And awaiting me back in my warm hotel was a little birthday party, a winter ale, and a football game. I also knew I'd soon return to Bear Lake, this time for the cisco.

~~~

Scott Tolentino, the Bear Lake fisheries biologist, stood outside my motel room on a January day, the air chilly but without the brutal winds of my previous trip. "The cisco weren't along shore yet yesterday, but I have a good feeling about today," he said. "There's wind blowing in, though, so we better get going."

We drove along the eastern side of the lake, to the appropriately named Cisco Beach. A couple of other trucks were parked nearby, with a few people heading to the beach in the dark. We would attempt netting them this morning, the traditional method of cisco capture. Fishermen use long-handled dip nets, scooping into massive schools of spawning fish.

"We don't need the nets yet, let's just see if they're here," Tolentino said. "If they're going to show, it will be sunrise to around 9:30."

He shined his light into the water but no cisco showed. "If they're here, you'll catch your limit in fifteen minutes," he said.

The cisco might be in the deeper water just off the beach. While Tolentino has been studying Bear Lake fish extensively for more than twenty-five years, there are still mysteries. The endemic species also pose challenges for anglers. With its unique fish species and ecology, Bear Lake requires different thinking and approaches.

Most of the cisco netters immediately recognized Tolentino, and they began walking over to chat him up. A few asked if he wanted to check their licenses, but he shook his head. "I just like to know how everyone's doing," he said.

Later he would tell me that as important as the research is on the lake, public relations is equally so. The managing agencies from Utah and Idaho have to work together to manage species unfamiliar to most anglers. Given the history of fisheries management in the United States, this would seem the perfect recipe for agency infighting and distrust. But here, the managers work closely together and local anglers take great pride in catching (and often eating) the local specialties.

Tolentino walks along the beach, looking into the shallows one more time. "They're not going to be here today," he said. "Let's get the boat."

Ice covers Bear Lake three out of every four years. During icy years, large holes are cut in the ice for netting ciscos. Other anglers use more conventional ice fishing techniques. When it's open water, cisco can be caught from boats with rod and reel, but even this fishing is a bit unconventional.

Tolentino made the mistake of asking me to back the boat down the ramp. After five tries, he recognized the futility and backed it in himself, and we motored a few minutes to an area known as the "rock pile." It would not have been hard for even a novice to find, as four other boats gathered within a 100-yard radius, the only boats in sight. Anglers dangled lines straight over, jigging them up and down.

As we pulled up, guys from each boat called out greetings. "All these guys are friends," Tolentino said.

A cheerful mood prevailed, and soon it was easy to see why. Nearly every cast brought up cisco. One man let out an excited yelp as his rod doubled over; he reeled up a large cutthroat.

Tolentino handed me a rod rigged with a one-ounce yellow jig, about half the size of the cisco. He explained the technique: You drop the jig straight down to the bottom and then begin jigging it about a foot, up and down. The cisco gather along the rock pile in astonishing numbers, and swim up to the yellow jig with thoughts of spawning on their mind (cisco develop a colorful yellow streak during mating season). As the jig moves up, it snags the cisco, and you reel it up.

My preference, like many anglers, is to "fair catch" fish in their mouths—to fool them into biting on bait, lure, or fly. Indeed, many anglers I encountered in the course of this book firmly believed—on an almost religious level—that fair catching was the *only* way to fish. Others believed only fly fishing could really qualify as real sport. I understand, but I've never found purism to be a recipe for fun. I brought along tiny flies and hooks to try to lure in cisco along shore. This would have been tough; they're plankton eaters. But the cisco on the rock pile were in 50 feet of water, rendering the use of tiny flies impossible. Ultimately, I wanted to experience the traditional fishery. Plus, cisco snagging is fun.

We both let our lines drop to the bottom. Within two twitches, Tolentino brought up a cisco. He dropped his rod down and almost immediately had another. He guessed I wasn't all the way on the bottom. I let more line out, felt a bump, lifted up and had a fish on. I brought it to the surface, a cisco hooked neatly in the lip.

The ciscos Tolentino had caught were silvery, resembling long sardines. They were torpedo-like, with small mouths and a pointy head. My first one was starting to develop red and yellow sides, and was covered with tubercles—small bumps. It was a fish in spawning glory, and a striking little species to catch.

I lowered my rod again, jigged, and had another one. I got the rhythm and soon we were both pulling in one cisco after another. At one point, a fish wriggled off at the surface. The cisco struggled to right itself and return to the deep, but remained a minute too long: a bald eagle swooped in, splashed the water's surface and gulped it down.

I dropped my line back in the water, and kept catching, and catching. Nothing else existed but the jig and the fish, until Tolentino said, "We better start counting."

The limit is thirty cisco per person, and we were at forty-five. I looked up and noticed ominous clouds rolling in. We let out our lines. On the next cast, Tolentino's rod twitched a little more than usual. "A whitefish," he said.

As he pulled it on board, it was a Bear Lake whitefish, yet another endemic species in the lake. While similar to the Bonneville whitefish, it was smaller with a more compact look. Tolentino showed me how to count scales above the fish's lateral line to accurately determine species: the Bear Lake whitefish has a line of eight scales from the lateral line to the top of the back, while the Bonneville has nine or ten.

And then, the action stopped. We still had eight fish to go, and the wind was picking up. "A predator must be passing through," Tolentino said.

The action soon resumed. Tolentino wanted the full allotment, as he would be frying them up as part of the festivities for the weekend's Cisco Disco. As I put the final fish of my limit into the livewell, a strong blast of wind sent ripples across the water.

"Time to go," Tolentino said. We blasted toward shore, and I noticed other boats pulling anchor, too.

We returned to the Bear Lake fisheries office—basically a trailer—and quickly cut off the heads, gutted, and scaled the fish. I got back to my little motel room and stretched out for a minute. I had been recovering from a particularly nasty bout of the flu, and my eyes were showing signs of conjunctivitis. I immediately drifted off to sleep with cisco dancing in my head.

Bear Lake's native fisheries may be thriving, but there are still challenges, of course. In the recent past, the biggest concern, according to Tolentino, was septic systems in the homes and businesses that line the lake. Most of those are now on a sewage system.

Extended drought could pose a more significant challenge, especially if climate change leads to warmer and drier winters. But Bear Lake's 2018 water levels were the highest since 1911, when measurements began.

Bear Lake is a natural water body, but a diversion from the Bear River runs into the lake. This water is allocated for irrigation by Rocky Mountain Power. The top 21 feet of the lake's water is allocated for this purpose.

Since many native fish spawn close to shore, if water levels dropped significantly, the eggs of species like the Bear Lake sculpin could be left high and dry during a drought. In the 1990s, irrigators, state agencies, and a group called Bear Lake Watch began meeting to hash out water use. Those early meetings were tense.

"Bear Lake Watch was considered tree huggers," says Tolentino. "The irrigators sat on one side and Bear Lake Watch on the other. It was polarized."

Although in the current political climate it seems almost delusional to think this contentiousness could end, people at the meetings continued to show up and listen. And as they worked through issues, the sides began to see reasons for agreement.

"Now everyone is at the same table. It's a friendly atmosphere, completely different," says Tolentino.

And irrigators voluntarily take cuts to their water based on projections, ensuring adequate water for the lake. Nobody wins if the lake levels drop and fish populations decline. If a species in Bear Lake became endangered, it would mean more severe water cuts for irrigators, restrictions for development, and restrictions for recreational fishing. "Nobody wants that," says Tolentino. "The fish are doing well. We want to keep it like that. It's a unique situation in many ways."

I woke up the next morning ready to search for cisco again, on my own this time. I had gotten some antibiotics for my eyes at a local clinic, and they were clearing up. I headed out in the dark to Cisco Beach. Waves lapped at the surface and wind-whipped trees, once again less-than-optimal conditions. I looked around but could see no cisco. A few netters stood along the banks, staring into the water.

I spent the morning casting lures for cutthroat trout to no avail. I decided to spend the afternoon targeting lake trout, a non-native species stocked in the lake. This seemed a bit of an anomaly in a lake that still basically has its functioning ecosystem. Both Utah and Idaho stocked fertile lake trout in this lake for nearly a hundred years, and the fish never became established. The unique water quality in the lake, plus the abundant endemic species that feast on lake trout eggs, made Bear Lake the only lake in the Western United States where lake trout were introduced without becoming a long-term problem. The infertile fish stocked today pose extremely low risk.

The Bear Lake Fisheries Management Plan seeks to balance sport fishing needs and also native fish conservation. "We have trigger levels for all the native species. If they begin to decline, we change management," Tolentino says. "We can reduce or eliminate lake trout stocking."

Darin Pugmire, who owns the largest sporting goods store on the lake, believes that there should be more stocking, not less. "This fishery is very difficult for people to figure out," he says. "A lot of the shore fishing takes place in winter. It's specialized. Rainbow trout could be stocked and provide a summer shore fishery. They could stock sterile rainbows, just like they do with lake trout."

And so the balancing act for managers goes. There is not a viable guiding industry on the lake, and while I see anglers every day, it's hardly crowded. I'd rather the lake's management focus solely on native fish, but many anglers want to catch a truly big fish. And the lake trout, stuffed on cisco and whitefish, can be monstrous.

I returned to the Bear Lake Marina, where I had caught my Bonneville whitefish, for a lake trout excursion. I had seen anglers there yesterday using ciscos for bait. I sank two hooks into a dead cisco, one in the head and one in the tail.

I cast out from the rocks. The water looked blue, almost Caribbean. I sat and shivered and prepared for a long wait. Most lake trout, here and elsewhere, are caught by trolling, with boats dragging large lures and baits deep in the water. I was not sure of my prospects from shore.

I watched a pair of western grebes drift by and enjoyed the mountains looming in the distance. Despite the chilly conditions, I felt content. Just me, the rod, the waiting.

Had I been there twenty minutes? An hour? I lost track of time. I lost track of everything. But something suggested my rod had just twitched. Just as I was ready to write that off as the wind, it began a steady throbbing. I lifted up and my rod bent straight over. It wasn't quite the screaming drag of the outdoor magazines, but the fish took line. As I began reeling, it suddenly stopped, and the line slackened. I reeled madly, as I realized the fish was heading toward shore. Toward the big rocks.

I steered it away from a jagged boulder and soon had it along the bank. By lake trout standards, it wasn't a huge fish, but I was happy with the 8-pound fish. I unceremoniously bonked it on the head, and put it in the snow to keep for a later dinner. I understood why there were lake trout here, but I wasn't going to throw one back.

＊＊＊

Then came the Cisco Disco. The disco was part of the area's official winter festival, the Bear Lake Monster Winterfest. (Like many large lakes, Bear Lake is rumored to have its own aquatic monster, although its popularity seems to lag far behind Nessie.) The event features a polar plunge in the lake, a chili cook-off, and various raffles. But for me, and apparently others, the cisco netting took top priority.

This year, the cisco proved uncooperative. I made my way to the food booth at the disco, where Tolentino and others were already serving heaping plates of fried cisco, French fries, fried scones with honey butter, coleslaw, and potato salad. "A good healthy breakfast," he said with a laugh. A line was already beginning to form. I picked up a fried cisco and took a bite. The bones and skin crunched in my mouth, and I got a flavor burst of fishy goodness, like a fried herring snack. For many people, this is what brings them out year after year. Wild food, there for the taking. Most years. They'd show up, of course, just on their own time schedule.

By 8:30, it became clear that the fishermen would be skunked this year. A surprising number of netters remained in the icy water, up to their waists, as if summoning fish from the depths. Others gathered by picnic tables, snacking and telling stories. As I walked to my car, I stopped by one family laughing and obviously reliving past discos.

"The first year we came, we had no idea what we were doing," said Brian Christiansen, who had driven up from Salt Lake City. "We walked out to a hole in the ice and looked down. There were fish everywhere. We stuck in our nets and got limits. Just like that."

"We thought this was going to be easy, but then there's a year like this year," said his son, Mike. "But it gets you out with your family. Even when it's been five below, we come up here. What else would we be doing?"

CHAPTER EIGHT

A Sucker Star is Born

In the summer, the creek consisted of placid pools, gentle riffles, and clear water. On this April morning, I could only find frothing rapids and water turned a milky gray from churned sand and gravel. My first assessment concluded fishing would be futile. I stared, as if I could will the waters to subside.

Normally, I wouldn't have even looked this early in the year. The mountain creek, just a twenty-minute drive from home, waxes and wanes with the seasons. Come spring, snow melts off the adjacent mountains, sending torrents of cold water rushing toward Boise. This is the water that fills reservoirs, water that is carefully assessed and obsessed over by everyone from farmers to fish biologists. I've had seasons when this stream remained too high to fish well into June.

April was too early, I told my wife Jennifer earlier in the day. But I'd drive up and check anyhow, just in case. My initial pessimism didn't dissipate as I walked along the stream. As I looked closer, though, I saw a calm eddy here, a slower pool there. Maybe, just maybe, I could get a bait to hold in that current. I realized I was talking myself into fishing.

I felt more conflicted because I wasn't assessing conditions for a normal outing. Jennifer works for Zoo Boise, and the zoo was hosting an event with noted photographer Joel Sartore that night.

Sartore is best known as a National Geographic photographer; his latest all-consuming project is called Photo Ark, in which he is photo-documenting the world's biodiversity.

Most wildlife photography takes place in natural habitats, of course, but Sartore's Photo Ark takes a markedly different approach. He photographs zoo animals in makeshift studios, taking their images on white or black backgrounds. It's just the animal, and the effect is stunning. Audiences at his slideshow gasp at the beauty of often-overlooked wildlife, from four-toed jerboas to red-fanned parrots to pearl charaxes butterflies.

His goal is to photograph every species exhibited in zoos and aquariums around the globe, a total of some fifteen thousand species. He's photographed more than eight thousand as of this writing. He aims to catalog the astonishing biodiversity before it's gone. Many conservation biologists acknowledge we're in the midst of a sixth mass extinction in the planet's history, one that is wiping out many species before we even discover them. In fact, a number of species Sartore has photographed have already disappeared.

Most people know about the plight of giant pandas, tigers, and rhinos, but the bulk of the world's wildlife remains unappreciated, unknown, ignored. Like freshwater fish. The native trout species and subspecies covered in previous chapters may face uncertain futures, but at least they have a constituency of anglers who care. The astonishing array of North America's native fish lack any such constituency. Underwater, they're out of sight, out of mind.

Sartore is interested in capturing freshwater biodiversity in his Photo Ark, too. For his Boise trip, he had lined up a trip to a local nature center, but it fell through. He had a free morning and knew Idaho had some interesting, if unappreciated, native fish. As he wandered the offices of Zoo Boise, he wondered if anyone could show him some of the nearby fish species.

Jennifer thought that I could perhaps catch something in my favorite local fishing spot, a stretch of creek I love because it happens to contain a number of largely unknown and unappreciated native species, including a healthy population of large-scale suckers. Sartore promised to give any fish I caught the studio treatment along the stream. How could I refuse?

The only problem was, of course, the stream itself. I really wanted to make this work, but I didn't want to waste anyone's time. Especially not Sartore, one of my conservation heroes. I drove home and called Jennifer, giving her the dim prospects for procuring a native fish.

"What would you say the odds of catching something are?" she asked.

"Ten percent, at best," I replied.

"Well, it's either go out with us or he sits around the office checking emails all morning," she said.

I realized that his options mirrored mine. I too faced a day of meetings and endless emails. Or I could go fishing. The water may have been murky, but in the end the choice was crystal clear.

———

Almost everything you've ever heard about suckers is probably wrong. Not just wrong. Flat-out crazy wrong.

*They're dirty. Non-native. A sign of polluted water. Garbage eaters. **Egg** eaters. Not to mention horrifically ugly.*

They compete with native fish, like trout and bass. There are too many. They're overtaking the waters.

The best thing to do? Catch 'em and throw 'em on the bank. You'll be doing the stream a favor.

Joel Sartore may have an appreciation for suckers. Most anglers do not. One of the most anti-conservation and illogical tendencies of the fishing community is its treatment of "trash" fish (basically, any fish outside a small list of preferred "game" species). When you get right down to it, most anglers know very little about native fish or healthy streams. That may seem like a harsh assessment, but anglers' widely accepted war on non-game fish proves otherwise.

Suckers and other so-called "rough" fish have long been persecuted by both anglers and fisheries managers. The Western United States has a diversity of sucker species, and many of them are now among the most imperiled fish on the continent. This is due in large part to dams and dewatering rivers for irrigation, particularly in the Colorado River and its tributaries.

But suckers and other non-game species have long been targeted by anglers and fisheries managers for removal. Jen Corrinne Brown writes in her book, *Trout Culture*,

> *The ways in which many anglers, tourists and fish managers understood place—the West as a manufactured trouty place— turned out deadly for native, non-trout species. The poor treatment of native coarse fish (simply defined by Euroamerican angling culture as most other fish species besides trout and salmon) reveals a historical trend that began in the late nineteenth century and has continued, at least in part, until today.*

She notes that even Norman Maclean, who has achieved sainthood status among fly fishers for his classic *A River Runs Through It*, considered Montana's non-native rainbow trout to be almost spiritual creatures, while decrying the presence of native suckers and pikeminnows.

While attitudes in fisheries management have shifted to favor native species, many anglers have not kept up. They continue to throw fish on the bank, spear them, shoot them with bows, and in general treat these fish like trash. This is based not on science but on misplaced fishy prejudice.

I've always been interested in different species of fish, but several years ago I realized that my angling horizons remained somewhat limited. I would see suckers hugging the bottom but had no real idea how to fish for them. I decided to rectify that. And from my first day fishing for "rough" fish, I began to realize just how ignorant most anglers were about them.

On that bright February day, I stood on a footbridge overlooking crystal-clear springs, in my first attempt at Idaho's most common sucker, the largescale.

The suckers were highly visible; large fish congregated by the dozens. But my sucker reverie was soon interrupted. Within minutes, two different people approached me to share their sucker knowledge. As if they had a compulsion to do so. One was carrying a large spinning rod with PowerBait. The other looked like he stepped out of an Orvis catalog. Apparently, a hate of suckers transcends trout fishing styles.

The first, the bait guy, offered this: *"We call them pikeminnows, or carp. They're invasive."*

Three strikes here. Aside from some common game species, most anglers are happy to lump everything else together into one species. Like my new friend.

His short commentary was filled with error. To boot: Suckers are not pikeminnows, native fish with an image problem of their own (they're blamed for reducing salmon populations, never mind dams). Suckers definitely aren't carp, which actually *are* non-native species. Suckers are not invasive: seventy-eight of the some eighty species in the sucker family, Catosomidae, are found exclusively in North America.

I barely had time to respond when the second expert approached. *"Fishing for suckers, huh? Well, I don't think you're going to catch them here. The water's too clean. They only live in polluted streams. They eat garbage. That's what I heard."*

OK, let's think about this carefully for a second: *The. Water. Is. Too. Clean.*

Here we must confront the most common of sucker myths: that this is a fish so vile it actually needs our pollution, our sediment, our trash. It's also totally, completely wrong. If you think about it, the idea makes no sense. No fish *needs* dirty water (no, not even carp). For many sucker species, it's quite the opposite. They need the purest, cleanest water. They need healthy river habitats. They need free-flowing stream so they can make their spring spawning run—just like other, more celebrated migratory fish. The sucker, ultimately, is the perfect symbol for healthy rivers and fisheries. Still, the myths persist. One has only to look at fishing social media sites to see all the vitriol aimed at suckers and other non-game species. Take this selection of comments about sucker fishing on a site called BigFish Tackle:

"Kill and through [sic] back."

"If you catch them while trying to catch trout of coarse [sic] they are in direct competition with the trout. They eat the same thing. There is only so much food and if the suckers are eating it. Less food for the trout."

"yeah a good slice to the belly or a few puncture wounds to pop there [sic] air bladder works great for a catch and release on those suckers and carp!!!!"

"I have a close friend who is a biologist . . . He simply slices open the belly and returns them back to the water. His theory is they will be food for something. And wont [sic] be eating the fish we have come there to catch. Side note. . . Look at Big Springs in Island Park. Huge suckers in there now . . . Makes me sick"

What makes me sick is that attitudes like this still exist. In the sportsmen's echo chamber, such ecological illiteracy passes as fact and even science. To someone on the outside looking in, such sentiments and actions appear wasteful, cruel, and unjustifiable.

To be fair, the non-angling community is not exactly picking up the banner for sucker conservation. In fact, if we're going to grow native fish appreciation, it's likely going to come from people who fish. Is it too much to ask for anglers to embrace suckers as the great game fish they are, for the sporting community to ask suckers to be managed with the same level of attention as bass and trout? I don't think so. In fact, I have seen the future, and it's for suckers.

I don't say this because I envision a future where bass and trout have been wiped out, and the postapocalyptic fly fisher will be reduced to casting to rough fish. Instead, I see a future where anglers embrace all fish, both as vital parts of healthy waters and as great quarry.

The rough fish revolution may not be televised, but it sure has benefited from online and social media. Sure, there have been books celebrating the virtues of overlooked native fish, most notably Ron Buffler and Tom Dickson's *Fishing for Buffalo* (buffalo are beefy and somewhat challenging-to-catch sucker species found in the Midwest and South). But online sites have allowed native fish appreciators to share tips, trade trips, and revel in the intricacies of sucker identification. Leading the way is Roughfish.com, a site created by Minnesota brothers Drew Geving and Corey Geving, devoted to the principle that "all fish species deserve respect." Most of the participants at Roughfish.com would take a sucker over a brown trout, any day. The site offers meet-ups, contests, a feature that allows anglers to track their "life list" of species caught, and one of the more complete guides to the fish species of North America (far better than any resources I've seen from state agencies devoted to fish conservation).

While the Roughfish.com community and similar sites represent a small fraction of the angling community, it's a start. However, even many rough fishers acknowledge that one of the nice benefits of targeting suckers is that you often have waters all to yourself. I once traveled to a river in southeast Minnesota considered by many rough fish aficionados to be a blue-ribbon fishery for redhorse, a particularly hard-fighting and handsome family of sucker. I arrived during the redhorse spawning run, and spent the day battling tough fish after tough fish. Every few minutes I'd have reel-screaming runs, fish that broke me off, fish that made my heart race. All this along rocky bluffs, hardwood forest and clear waters.

And not an angler in sight. Nine hours of prime fishing, and I didn't see a single human being carrying a fishing rod. It is if I showed up at the Madison River at the height of the salmon fly hatch and had the whole river to myself.

The impulse, of course, is to guard this secret. Let others ignore suckers; it just means we can have that exceedingly rare combination of great fishing *and* solitude. But to state fisheries managers, that solitude looks an awful lot like lack of interest. And that lack of interest means a lack of license sales. It also means no one's going to stop bowfishers from shooting hundreds of suckers with a bow in your favorite stream, leaving their rotting carcasses lining the bank. In fact, that's perfectly legal and acceptable in many states.

Cutthroat trout are being reintroduced and restored to many streams in their native range, all because fly rodders support the effort. They're completing those Cutt Slams and posting those photos on Instagram. Sure, some anglers still prefer non-native brown trout. But the opposition to restoring cutthroats is nothing compared to restoring the West's native suckers. If more anglers joined the rough fish renaissance, maybe we could one day cast a worm to razorback suckers in the Colorado River, or perhaps stalk a Klamath sucker in Oregon. Dare to dream. Gila trout conservation plunges ahead in no small part because there are streams where people can fish for them. Razorback sucker conservation struggles, and angling is prohibited. Evenif streams were set aside where anglers could target reintroduced populations, the perception is no one would care.

As I stand along the river fighting a silver redhorse with a simple ultralight rod, slip sinker and worm, I'll admit that I don't want an army of anglers joining me. I don't want the inevitable commercialization, the fancy gear, rivers leased up by guides. But if we want river management to focus on all native species, we need more people fishing for suckers.

Joel Sartore, of course, has his own way to get people fired up about biodiversity. He's reaching literally millions through his National Geographic articles, online photos, books, and presentations. And now, he wanted a sucker.

The morning after Sartore's presentation, our fishing expedition got off to a late start. I loaded just about any conceivable piece of fishing gear to ensure success, while Jennifer loaded every conceivable snack item to ensure our toddler son, Derek, didn't have a meltdown. I wanted to get to the creek early, just to feel things out before Sartore arrived. But with Derek's usual dawdling, we arrived at the little national forest pull-off just a few minutes before Jennifer's supervisor, Rachel Winer, pulled in with Sartore. He looked over my fishing gear but didn't seem overly concerned by my pessimistic predictions.

"I don't need a big one, just a fish," he told me. "In fact, smaller is better."

He then set off downstream to sift through vegetation and rocks for aquatic invertebrates. Jennifer, meanwhile, filled buckets with water so they'd be ready in case I landed a fish. I stared again at the rushing water. On my first cast, the current whipped my weight and bait downstream. I cast again, just a few feet out where a back eddy swirled. My steel weight held, and I waited.

Five minutes passed. Based on many previous sucker fishing outings at this spot, I knew that if the fish were around, they bit quickly. Maybe it would take them longer to find the worm in this swift current, I reasoned to myself. Sartore emerged from downstream with a bucket of caddis fly larvae in their little stone casings, as well as some stonefly nymphs. At least the morning wouldn't be a total bust.

I cast to another spot upstream. The weight caught on the bottom, and the line sat there. Another five minutes passed. My line ticked. The current? I reeled in, and the worm was gone. I forced the flicker of hope away. It could have been dislodged by a stick. I rebaited and cast to the same spot.

Again my line ticked. Once, twice. I lifted . . . and felt a solid weight. I set the hook and reeled and felt a solid surge into the heavy current.

"Fish on!" I yelled. "Get the bucket!"

Jennifer, with Derek on her back, sprang into action. I fought the fish gingerly, careful not to lose it. Then I swung it toward the bank, and gently plopped it into the bucket. A beautiful footlong specimen of a largescale sucker drifted there. I slipped the barbless hook out of its mouth, and Jennifer raced downstream to get Sartore.

He was all smiles as he came bounding up. He looked down at the fish in the bucket. "Beautiful," he said. "OK, I'm going to go get set up for photos. You keep fishing. See if you can catch a smaller one."

That's the first time I've received that particular instruction, but I baited up again and cast out. Sartore, meanwhile, set up a canopy under which he placed a fish tank and his camera and flash, with lighting supplied by a portable generator.

Before he completed his temporary studio by the stream, my rod bucked again. This time when I lifted up, I saw a fish dart across a riffle and head downstream, peeling off line. It was not a smaller fish. In fact, it may well have been the biggest largescale sucker I've ever caught in this spot. For all the detractors of suckers as game fish, many species fight hard, largescale suckers among them. With a fish already in the bucket, I felt less pressure this time, and patiently played the fish. I finally landed it, and placed it in a second bucket, where I could see a beautiful sucker in bright, breeding color—a dark olive back making its namesake large scales shine, with a bright yellow belly. Sartore walked down and looked the fish over. Despite its large size, it was too beautiful not to photograph.

This fish became perhaps the most photographed largescale sucker in history. We placed it gently in the photo tank, trying both white and black backgrounds. I'd lift it gently from its belly, and it would drift to the bottom of the tank, Sartore snapping away with his camera. At one point, he got even closer, focusing just on the head.

"I want to show its sucker mouth," he said.

The sucker mouth. How much of the sucker's bad reputation comes from that low-slung mouth, looking like a suction cup? Is that why anglers imagine it suctions trout eggs from the bottom? Is it why people assume it eats garbage?

But seen with fresh eyes, it's just a fish perfectly adapted to these Rocky Mountain streams. That mouth scrapes algae and invertebrates off rocks. The olive back allows the sucker to hide among those rocks, concealing it from ospreys and eagles. Its stout body allows it to fin in riffles even when snowmelt rushes off the mountain.

It's a perfect fish, if only we can see. It's what keeps Sartore going, setting up studios wherever he travels. We all stood there oohing and ahhing over a sucker. But can efforts like the Photo Ark and Roughfish.com really chart a brighter future for native fish? Could anglers, even the public, really come to love suckers?

The photo shoot complete, I walked the bucket back down to the creek, releasing our sucker "model" into the cold, rushing water. A contentedness settled over our little group, as so often happens after a successful fishing trip. Derek played in the sand with his Tonka trucks and mussel shells he found along the streambank. Sartore shifted his attention to caddis flies. Jennifer broke out some donuts. I cast out my line, and soon hooked up with another fish.

The next evening, I glanced at Facebook, and on the Southwest Idaho Fishing group, saw a photo of an angler hoisting a sucker. The first comment: "I always stomp on their head, and throw them on the bank for the foxes."

At times, educating anglers about the value of native fish seems the definition of futility. But sometimes native rough fish make the transition to sport fish. In Texas, in fact, a trophy catch-and-release fishery had started for a fish persecuted with even more vigor than suckers. What happens when trash becomes trophy? It was time to head south for some river monsters.

Chapter Nine

Gar Wars: The Cast of the Drones

Bubba stood on the boat deck, his logo-covered performance fishing shirt splattered with fish guts. One hand held a drone over his head; his other grasped a large treble hook attached to my line.

"Hand me a carp head," he said.

My friend Solomon David reached into the cooler and quickly delivered the head to Bubba. He embedded the treble hook into the carp, then clipped the drone onto the fishing line. He reached down and picked up his remote control and pressed a button as the drone took off with its unconventional cargo.

I held the heavy spinning rod, the line reeling out freely. The drone flew 100 yards across the bayou to a slight channel, then hovered.

"Drop the carp," Bubba ordered.

I clicked the reel and gave a short but sharp jerk. The carp head detached, fell to the surface and disappeared, leaving a large bobber floating. As Bubba piloted the drone back to the boat, Solomon got another rod ready for a new bait. Within a few minutes, six fish heads bobbed in the bayou.

We sat down, watching the bobbers. One began to bounce as it drifted into the center of the bayou; another jerked, then stopped, jerked, then stopped. In nearly any other fishing situation,

Solomon and I would be on the rods, ready to set the hook. Today, the target was alligator gar, one of the largest freshwater fish in North America. With a long snout and pointy teeth, it shakes and chews its prey first. To hook it, you have to make sure it has fully taken the bait. And so you wait, and wait. The bobber drifts, the bobber bobs, and still you wait.

The line flowed steadily from the reel but without tension. As we watched, one line began moving faster, skimming the bobber across the surface. The fish was on the move, and it had swallowed the bait.

Bubba nodded, pointed at me. "Hit 'im," he said.

I stood up, lifted the rod, and pulled back in a fluid motion. More than 100 yards away, a fish boiled and began peeling even more line. The fight was on. I allowed the fish to take line, but the second it hesitated, I'd lean back and strain against the weight.

Slowly, slowly, I drew the fish closer to the boat. "Forty pounder," said Bubba, dismissively.

A fish-of-a-lifetime in nearly any other river on the continent, but here one hardly worth mentioning, at least not by Bubba. Nonetheless, the fight grew more frantic as I drew the fish closer to the boat. Suddenly, it burst into the air, shaking its head and spraying water. It jumped again. I whooped like the host of a bass fishing show. Solomon clicked away with his camera.

The aerial show stopped and the gar finned in the water. Bubba grabbed two rope nooses, slipped them over the gar's head and tail, and hoisted it into the boat. Gar, plated with armor and able to gulp oxygen from the air, fare better than most fish species when roughly handled.

I put the fish on my lap for a few more photos, then dropped it overboard. I wiped my hands, and saw another bobber moving across the bayou. "You're up, Solomon," Bubba said.

Solomon stood on the bow, bent his legs and readied for the fight. As he set the hook, the line surged. "That's a much better one," Bubba said.

This fight didn't involve aerial acrobatics, just brute force as 5 feet of gar surged through the bayou, leaving Solomon exclaiming and swearing until finally, it, too, was in the boat. Solomon beamed as he stared at the 80-pounder at his feet.

He grinned, and looked up at me. "GARgantuan," he said.

～～

The alligator gar is one of seven gar species, five of which reside in the United States. They're an ancient fish lineage that swam with dinosaurs. They've survived asteroids and other global calamities, but as with so many species, now face what is perhaps their toughest test.

I first learned of gar in childhood, even though the Central Pennsylvania waters near my home didn't have any. I loved obscure wild animals of all kinds. Yes, I explored the local creeks and woodlots near me, but Marlin Perkins's *Wild Kingdom* and a diet of nature and outdoor books and magazines filled my head with more exotic beasts. I loved kudus and anacondas and cassowaries. A guidance counselor advised me in junior high that if I continued my interests in subjects like ground squirrels, I'd be lucky to ever amount to more than the county dog catcher (I actually didn't think this sounded like a bad option). I continued on my path. The more bizarre the creature, the better I loved it.

One day, I paged through a fishing book at the local library and came across a photo of an alligator gar. The fish certainly bore a resemblance to an alligator, as it was covered with large scales and had a long, pointy snout with fearsome-looking teeth. Another childhood book, called *Fish Do The Strangest Things*, featured an illustration of a gar actually chomping an alligator. This was fanciful; gar may look imposing but they'd be unlikely to take on a full-size gator. But such a gnarly fish fueled my dreams. As I researched, several books mentioned that gar were not "sport fish." I didn't care. I wanted to see this fish firsthand.

I got my chance years later during a year living in rural southern Kansas. On a spring day, I visited a river a short drive from my home, a rented little farmhouse on the prairie. I hoped to find bass, but was even more excited when I saw a huge gathering of gar, stacked like logs near the water's surface. I cast a Rapala, a wobbling lure that resembled a minnow. Immediately a fish hit, and I missed. I cast again. A hit and miss.

Provided the water's warm, gar may be the least selective fish that swim. They'll attack lures or baits with reckless abandon. But given that bony snout, they're difficult to hook. To some, this lowers their appeal. To me, it's part of the great fun of gar fishing.

I caught several shortnose gar that day, reminding me of those childhood fish books. These gar were 20 inches or so, and put up a good fight on an ultralight spin rod—but they were miniatures compared to the big alligator gar that initially captured my attention.

I began to learn that many others didn't share the love. For decades, gar have been loathed not only as rough fish but also reviled as aggressive predators that gobble up more desirable species. They have even been accused of attacking humans.

As with other native rough fish, these rumors don't contain a shred of scientific fact. That didn't matter. Even fisheries managers for much of the 20th century encouraged aggressive gar control. People shot them with rifles, poisoned them, electrocuted them. The Gar Wars.

For the alligator gar, large and slow to mature, removing large numbers of fish coupled with habitat loss proved devastating. They disappeared from some states, like Illinois, and existed in vastly reduced numbers in many others.

And then came a new development in the Gar Wars: bowfishing. Bowfishing—quite simply, shooting fish with a bow—has been a niche outdoor sport for a long time. In the early 2000s, though, it began to achieve new popularity, as enthusiasts targeted rapidly proliferating Asian carp. These invasive fish spread rapidly up the

Mississippi and other Midwest river systems. They earned infamy for their habit of jumping high out of the water when disturbed by boat motors. Viral YouTube videos showed thousands of carp dancing across the surface. Some smashed into hapless boaters.

For archers, this proved a gigantic, guilt-free shooting gallery. Outdoor magazines published article after article about shooting flying carp. And who could object to controlling an invasive species?

The problem was, bowfishing regulations still allowed unlimited take of many native "rough" fish: the suckers, bowfin, and gar. Buffalo, a beefy sucker, look an awful lot like carp. Many rough fish, including gar, often congregate in large numbers. The bowfishers pointed their arrows at the natives with equal abandon and justified it as controlling "trash fish."

Bowfishing tournaments proliferated, and prizes were awarded not only for carp but for buffalo and gar as well. Bikini bowfishing calendars featured buxom blondes with gar skewered by arrows. Rough fish lovers visited their favorite streams, only to find the banks covered in the rotting, reeking carcasses of suckers and gar.

The alligator gar became the bowfisher's big game trophy. These fish can reach 7 feet or more. On the Trinity River in Texas, where some of the biggest gar still swim, a small guiding industry popped up, getting clients close to giant fish which they then shot. The hero photos featured smiling sportsmen standing next to three or five large, slow-growing fish. Often, those fish ended up in dumpsters.

Bubba was one of the best of those bowfishing guides. He guided Johnny Morris, founder of Bass Pro Shops and an early advocate of catch-and-release bass fishing, who shot and killed an 8-foot, 3-inch alligator gar. Bubba earned a reputation as a guy who knew the gar and how to kill them.

Years later came a different request, this time from Jeremy Wade of the cable show *River Monsters*. Wade wanted to film an episode of catch-and-release alligator gar fishing. Accompanied by Mark Spitzer, an author of gonzo gar fishing books, the two signed on with Bubba for part of their adventure.

It changed Bubba's career and life, although it wasn't quite a burning-bush conversion to catch-and-release angling. "I didn't really hit it off with Wade and Spitzer," he said. "They were tree huggers. We didn't see eye to eye on much of anything."

But Wade's show brought attention and lots of potential clients, anglers who saw an exciting big-game rod-and-reel fishing opportunity. They were willing to pay for the privilege to the tune of $650 per day. Bubba put down his bow and began exclusively doing catch-and-release trips.

I'm well aware of the critiques of Wade's show, the pulpy sensationalism, the potential for man-eating fish around every river bend, the shaky *Blair Witch* camera work to add drama. I have friends who deride Wade as a showman more than an angler or conservationist. But he also has the potential to bring attention to embattled fish, to ignite an interest in protecting them in a way that environmental organizations could only dream of replicating. His shows contain a conservation message and what appears a genuine love of fish.

In the Gar Wars, there's a new hope growing, as conservationists and anglers advocate for these ancient fish. Is *River Monsters* solely responsible? Absolutely not. But it certainly played an important role in jump-starting interest in giant alligator gar, particularly on the Trinity River.

When it came time for my own Trinity River trip, I knew who I wanted as a fishing partner: the ultimate "garficionado," Solomon David. He's now an aquatic ecologist and assistant professor at Nicholls State University in Louisiana. To call Solomon a gar researcher is like calling Lebron James a basketball player.

Solomon nets gar, dissects gar, raises them in aquaria. He has collections of gar toys, T-shirts, and skulls. He keeps them as pets. And he promotes them on social media in a whir of photos and gar puns. He hosted legendary parties (garties?) in his graduate school days at the University of Michigan that culminated with a gar feeding. "Wherever you go, there you gar," his Twitter profile reads.

Solomon, the son of first-generation Indian immigrants in Ohio, grew up exploring creeks and catching turtles. Then one day, he opened a *Ranger Rick* magazine and saw a picture of an ancient, toothy fish swimming through the bayou. He began to follow the gar, wherever the fish took him.

I met Solomon at the Shedd Aquarium, where at the time he was a research associate. We had been corresponding for more than a year, initiated by a piece I had written on his favorite fish. At the aquarium, we checked out the research facilities and the impressive gar exhibit. But most of all, we talked all things fish. I mentioned the budding idea I had for a trip after the really big gar in Texas, a road trip to see those river monsters firsthand and do plenty of fishing.

"Gar Trek," Solomon said.

"Interested?"

"Count me in," he said. "It will be an extravGARganza."

The trip itself didn't quite start out that way, as we spent the first four hours of Gar Trek staring at floating balloons. Bubba had met us at our hotel in the small town of Elkhart, Texas, his truck festooned with enough corporate logos to qualify for NASCAR. Bubba, unshaven and rumpled, nevertheless sported similarly bedazzled pro-gear from head to toe. Alligator gar, it appeared, had moved from rough status to full-on glamor fish, attracting sponsors, specialized gear and high-dollar guides.

Bubba wanted to check out a lake he hadn't visited in two years, rumored to contain truly monster gar. We launched a boat, and while those giant fish never materialized, we got our first look at the somewhat-bizarre world of trophy gar fishing.

Bubba's boat was lined with large, sturdy, red balloons, each tied to a fishing line that ended in a treble hook and a baited buffalo (the fish, not the mammal) or carp head. The balloons were dumped overboard, unattached to a fishing rod. Bubba scattered them around the lake. If a balloon began moving, he'd drive up to it in the boat, and loop the line attached to the balloon to a fishing rig. The angler would then set the hook and battle the fish. It resembled a jug line—a traditional method in the South where anglers set out fishing lines attached to plastic bottles and other floating objects. It allowed someone to cover a lot more water. It also meant that the angler was not actively fishing, just waiting for balloons to move.

We sat in the middle of the reservoir, Bubba periodically scanning the balloons with binoculars. As we sat, he regaled us with stories of fishing celebrities; since *River Monsters* aired, a long list of other fishing shows from across the globe had filmed with him. Eventually, talk turned to a rival gar guide on the river, with which Bubba had a running and increasingly bitter feud. This was in part competition; both guides regularly produced trophy gar, including world records, for their clients. It frequently turned nasty, spilling over into personal attacks on Facebook, accusations of stealing each others' clients, accusations of sketchy methods.

Bubba proclaimed that he knew more about gar than any other guide, a claim that seemed a bit hyperbolic given that we were sitting in a boat, watching balloons bob in place. Eventually, he admitted this experiment was a bust, and promised us a better afternoon. We picked up the balloons, motored across the lake and headed toward our next stop. After a quick break for fried chicken at a local convenience store, we arrived at a boat ramp set in what could have passed for a Hollywood jungle, where Bubba assured us the gar were thick. We set off and he dropped balloons as we drove.

I loved the thick vegetation lining the banks, the feeling of being in the tropics. Herons squawked as they launched into the air. Solomon looked antsy. He wanted gar time. We both had spent enough time around fish to know never to count on success, but we also both really wanted to see one of these Trinity River gar up close.

When the last balloon landed in the water, Bubba turned the boat around to head back up the line of baits. We cruised along, scanning each balloon. Suddenly, he slowed down. "That one has moved across the channel," he said.

Solomon graciously allowed me to go first, and I stepped up, grabbed the rod, and set the hook. I felt resistance, although not as much as I expected. "A baby one," Bubba said.

I reeled in a 12-pound alligator gar, my first of this species. I couldn't be happier. Just seeing the fish up close, touching its scales, staring in its eye . . . that was enough. We released it and moved on, and soon we entered a state of garvana: balloons moving and fish on.

Solomon followed next with a 35-pounder, a beautiful fish, and I quickly caught a similar-sized one. Bubba decided it was time to leave this narrow channel, so we picked up the remaining balloons and cruised into a more open area, like a small lake. "It's time to use the drone," he said.

I own up to having Luddite tendencies; I'll use technology but hardly qualify as an early adopter. A drone for fishing struck me as even more questionable than using balloons. Solomon, on the other hand, appeared to be levitating. Drones and primitive fish proved a happy combination. Admittedly, once the drones began casting our lines for us, I decided to roll with it.

We tangled with gar the rest of the afternoon. At one point, Solomon hooked a trophy—likely more than 100 pounds—but in its last dash, it took off directly under the boat and snapped him off. His normally upbeat demeanor dissipated . . . for about fifteen seconds. Then it was back to fishing. There were more river monsters out there.

The sun began to set, and Bubba took us to our lodging for the night. He had offered this over the phone a few nights before the trip. "You can stay there for free, but it's nothing fancy," he said. "It's a bit of a man cave. You may have to check the bed for spiders."

This, it turned out, was a wildly optimistic description of the little shack. I like roughing it. I have no aversion to cheap hotels and run-down cabins. But there's "nothing fancy" and then there's flat-out disgusting. Solomon and I soon realized we were the first guests to stay at the "cabin" this season, if not this decade. Two fully developed wasp nests were established *inside* the kitchen. The refrigerator was well-stocked with various jars and containers of food, but mold had overtaken all of them, and the fungi spread out of the containers onto the kitchen shelves. The bathroom served as a similar biodiversity hotspot.

We decided to go to town for dinner. We had to paddle a boat across the bayou to reach our rental car. The only viable option open was Applebee's, which never tasted so good or seemed so inviting. I don't think either of us wanted to leave. We paddled quietly back across the bayou in the dark. A feral pig began squealing in the distance.

"Deliverance," Solomon said.

The next morning, Bubba met us and unveiled a new plan. We'd go to another channel that connected to the Trinity, this one likely unfished in weeks. We hopped in the truck and drove across a swampy plain, arriving at a canal with grass higher than our heads. It was prison land, and the grass was usually mowed.

"I can't find where you back the truck in," Bubba said.

He took a guess, and a wrong one. The trailer sank in thick mud above the axles. We hopped out. Bubba shrugged, and began digging the truck out. By hand. We joined in, the ground growing harder and less willing to budge. The tedium of the task was not aided by that gnawing awareness that we were supposed to be fishing. Solomon began passing the time by blurting out obscure movie references and gar puns, sometimes combining the two, and often involving Gar Wars. A long time ago, in a galaxy gar, gar away. Garth Vader. Gar Gar Binks. That sort of thing.

Bubba tried to gun his truck, but the boat slid a bit on the bank, so that it now angled vertically over the river. He asked us to climb up to the bow of the boat, to hopefully provide some weight to pull it down. We dangled from the boat, keenly aware that we were spending $650 a day for this privilege. As Bubba revved his engine, the boat rocked precariously. Solomon started to slip and I grabbed his hand. We dangled at nearly a 90-degree angle.

"You go, we go," I said.

"*Backdraft*," Solomon said. "Not gar related, but points for the nineties' movie reference."

Finally, miraculously, Bubba extracted the trailer. It was nearly noon (in fairness, he has since offered us a complimentary day of gar fishing).

We returned to the bayou and spent that afternoon catching gar after gar. It almost was enough to forget about the morning. Almost.

—◦—

"If it pays, it stays" is a popular saying in global wildlife conservation. Particularly in the developing world, it can be difficult to argue with the sentiment. An elephant can destroy a farmer's entire crop overnight, making the animals destructive and unwelcome neighbors, worth more dead than alive. If, on the other hand, the elephant draws visiting tourists, that farmer can earn a better income, encouraging him to tolerate more elephants.

There's also something rankling, at least to some conservationists, about the underlying sentiment. The sentiment that suggests everything on earth has to have an economic value to survive.

The trophy gar fishery of the Trinity River undoubtedly benefits alligator gar. It makes those gar more valuable, and the Texas Department of Parks and Wildlife has passed more restrictive bowfishing regulations and limits as a result. While bowfishing remains wildly popular, catch-and-release fishing has become a viable alternative.

There are reasons to be hopeful for gar conservation beyond localized guiding industries. Solomon is a whirlwind of gar promotion, reaching both school kids and social media users with his infectious enthusiasm. There are still way too many people shooting these ancient fish with arrows and throwing them on the bank. But there are also signs of positive change.

Perhaps the most dramatic gar victory occurred in Illinois, not by coincidence the state where Solomon lived for several years. He and Jeff Stein of the Illinois Natural History Survey helped launch the Ancient Sport Fish Project that researches population trends for gar and bowfin, a project that continues to gather momentum and interest.

Then Illinois officially began a reintroduction program for alligator gar. This required a lot of public support, fueled by the efforts of Solomon and other passionate gar warriors like David Jakubiak of the Environmental Law and Policy Center and Olaf Nelson, a sucker and rough fish aficionado who runs a website called moxostoma.com.

The current effort did attract some opposition from a boating association, with sensationalistic claims that the alligator gar would attack children. But the reintroduction program was approved in 2016, and alligator gar are now being stocked in appropriate Illinois waters.

Even in mainstream outdoor publications, attitudes are changing. There are still articles that call gar "trash fish," of course. But it's becoming increasingly likely to also find stories celebrating them.

Johnny Carrol Sain wrote in *Hatch Magazine* about the time his wife asked if he had ever thought about his habit of bowfishing for gar.

"I had not. But I thought about it the next time a gar swam within range of my arrow," he writes.

He stopped bowfishing and, instead, reflected on mindless killing:

Of course gar die. Everything dies. But dead gar piled on the creek bank somehow seem outside the circle and its exquisite tragedy. The act of killing without thought or purpose runs counter to natural order. It may be one of the few true evils in this world.

For those of us who want a new angling reality in the 21st century: this is what progress looks like.

꙳

After our time with Bubba, Solomon and I had a free day to explore on our own. We decided to drive to a place called Richland Wildlife Management Area, reported to have healthy populations of longnose and spotted gar. We had about run out of water and snacks during our cabin stay, but figured we'd just stop for more along our drive. But the winding rural Texas road had few towns and nary a sight of a convenience store, so we figured we'd just fish for an hour or two and find a place for a break later. Why do I always believe I'll only be fishing for a short time?

As we drove, Solomon and I fell into easy conversation, not only about fishing but also about environmentalism, universities, football, movies, and more. Sometimes, it felt hard to believe that I had only spent four hours in person with him before this trip. Despite my misgivings about technology, I admit that I've met some of my finest friends via online media.

When we arrived, we found that Richland consisted of a series of canals and wetlands, most of the water quite shallow. A few pickup trucks lined the parking areas for the early duck-hunting season. The hunters concentrated on the larger ponds; we had the canals to ourselves. We rigged up our light travel rods and began casting—live worms, spinners, plugs—with no success whatsoever.

Meanwhile, duck hunters began filing out of the marsh, the high sun spelling the end of their outings. As I've come to expect when fishing for offbeat species in offbeat locations, we attracted attention. The duck hunters, it seemed, didn't think these little canals offered much in the way of fishing.

The first truck stopped around 10:00 a.m. A couple hopped out: young, attractive, fit, and dressed in stylish matching camo. They looked as if they had just stepped off the set of a hunting television show. He sported a coiffed goatee; his chiseled muscles rippled through his high-performance camo shirt. She had three streaks of finger-width camo carefully applied on each cheek, accented by cherry-red lipstick.

They were friendly, happy, and genuinely curious about our doings. "Gar?" the guy asked. "I thought people only shot them?'

Solomon patiently explained why gars were cool. He told them about the big ones we had caught on the previous days. How we had traveled from across the country for this experience.

Perhaps they drove off ready to tell their friends about the two out-of-state whack jobs fishing for gar. Or maybe they'd return next week with some fishing rods.

But our gar advocacy aside, we still hadn't caught one here. By late afternoon, we had run out of water and all our food except two apples. We decided to call it a day. Then an old truck sputtered to a stop. This guy wore a sleeveless shirt and greasy hat. He was unlikely to be confused as a cable television star, outdoor or otherwise.

"What are y'all doing?" the man hollered out.

"Gar fishing."

He slowly drove away, but five minutes later he came rumbling back. "OK, do you mind if I ask another question?" he asked.

"Go for it," I said.

"*Why* are y'all gar fishing?"

Solomon gave his answer and the man seemed surprised. Then he told us where we should be fishing, a dike system just a short drive away.

I was nearly delirious from dehydration and hunger. I looked at Solomon. "Let's give it a try, just for a few minutes."

These are always dangerous words, because it's never a few minutes. Not when you're obsessed with the outdoors.

We got to the spot and it indeed was filled with gar. We saw plenty of smaller forms—spotted and longnose gar—but in the shadows something much larger loomed. Alligator gar. I had only brought light tackle on the trip, as I thought we'd only be targeting alligator gar with Bubba. This presented a potential problem.

"What do we do if we hook into one of the big ones?" Solomon asked.

"We'll worry about that if it happens," I replied.

It happened. Once again, gar proved eager to bite but, particularly with lures, difficult to hook.

We had had a lot of action with the smaller gar slashing our swimbaits, but had landed no fish. Then I retrieved a shad lure and suddenly saw a large shadow trailing. The shallow water erupted as my rod bent. Alligator gar!

I turned to Solomon. He was twisting toward me, his own rod equally bent. An alligator gar double.

The next few minutes were characterized by exclamations, expletives, thrashing gar, and pure chaos. Both of ours eventually broke off as we tried to get them to shore. That was fine by me. Just having a close encounter with these awesome predators was plenty.

Solomon wanted to touch one. He wanted a photo. But even he acknowledged our state of dehydration. We drove to get water and food, and a landing net. We returned, and within a few minutes, I hooked another alligator gar. All hell broke loose. I played the fish slowly and Solomon scooped him into the net. We posed for some photos and released the fish back into its lair.

The sun was setting on our Gar Trek. Solomon and I high-fived. It was far from the biggest gar of the trip, but it's the one I remember best. It swims through my memories, an ancient fish still among us in the 21st century. A river monster? Sure. If that's what it takes to save them. But also a fish anyone can encounter, in out-of-the-way swamps and canals, no drones or balloons required.

CHAPTER TEN

Microfishing Mania among the Life Listers

Say you're in Boise, Idaho, on a sweltering July day, and you're looking for a way to cool off. Everyone suggests you head to the Boise River, where you find a calm side channel lined by sand. Dozens of kids play in and along the water, building castles, playing with boats, and splashing each other. Parents dip toes in the river as they enjoy cold beverages. Rafters and tubers pull in to the calm spot to take a break. It's a pleasantly busy summer scene.

Then you notice a man hunched over in the corner of the pool, just yards away from the chaos. In one hand he holds what looks like a thin magic wand, with a strand of fishing line extending straight down to his feet. He stares at it. Waiting like a human heron.

That would be me.

You might then be tempted to approach me to ask what the hell I am doing. Don't be offended if I don't respond. It's not personal. Ask my wife. On one such outing, our two-year-old son fell into the river in this very spot, screaming in terrified panic. My wife quickly pulled him out. She looked over at me, standing 10 feet away, and I remained in the same heron position. Later, she would ask why I had not tried to rescue my son. I had no idea what she was talking about. I was too busy staring at a tiny fleck of worm at my feet, trying to catch a speckled dace, a fish about the size of my thumb.

Welcome to microfishing, a pursuit that puts a new spin on extreme angling. It's defined as fishing with hook and line for tiny species of fish, what most people (including other anglers) know simply as "minnows." Its dedicated adherents use specialized rods, size 32 hooks that are smaller than the J on this page and an 8x tippet that feels like a strand of human hair. Whereas many fishermen measure their fish, microfishers count anal fin rays to determine the precise shiner species.

At times, I've considered the concentration required in tempting a small fish to bite as close to meditation as I'm likely to get. At other times, I suspect that I concentrate so intently because if I stopped to think about what I'm doing, I might die of embarrassment.

I keep at it, if only because it makes me feel like a kid again. I recall many a childhood fishless day spent at a state park lake, watching as schools of minnows swirled along shore. I tried to devise ways I could catch them on my trout tackle, but even the smallest hooks proved far too big.

Today, it would be a gross exaggeration to call microfishing a craze, but with online resources, like-minded nerds can share tips and tactics. There are microfishing blogs, videos, and Facebook groups. It has been featured as a human interest story in large newspapers. There is even a tackle supplier, Tenkara Bum, that offers the miniaturized rods, hooks, line, weights, and floats necessary to outfit yourself for minnow fishing.

Chris Stewart, owner of Tenkara Bum, notes on his blog that he sees his business jump every time microfishing is featured in another news story. "I suppose it is not surprising that most of this new interest is not coming from hard core fishermen," he writes on his blog. "It seems to be from people who fished as kids and gave it up or who fish a bit but never really got into it."

While it might seem novel here, microfishing has a long-established tradition in Japan. Japanese anglers pursue a variety of small fish using hook and line, including one tiny specimen called the tanago. The object of tanago fishing is to see how *small* a fish you can catch, with the grail being a tanago that can fit on a two-yen coin (about the size of a penny). This demands ultra-sensitive rods, tiny hooks and bait, and extreme levels of patience. US microfishing has grown in large part because of the availability and interest in Japanese fishing gear. Tenkara, a form of fishing involving a long rod and a line but no reel, has become a bona fide fad and is billed as "radically simple fly fishing." Tenkara rods are now available at most fly shops and even major outdoor retailers like Patagonia. They're usually used for trout fishing in mountain streams, not for catching minnows. But the attention also generated interest in other forms of Japanese fishing, including the micro gear.

I suspect it's more than the availability of gear fueling an interest in microfishing. Perhaps American anglers have begun pursuing shiners and sculpins because their pursuit is simply more accessible than fishing for trout or bass.

Let's consider Japan. The country has 127 million people crammed into an area half the size of Texas. Written accounts of tanago fishing often give the impression that its appeal lies in the meditative state and patience required to fool an elusive yet minuscule fish. But let's be honest: given the choice, most anglers would choose to pursue large, tasty fish. Japanese anglers pursue tanago because there are simply too many people for everyone to pursue large species.

Chief Sitting Bull famously said, "When the buffalo are gone, we will hunt mice, for we are hunters and we want our freedom."

In even the most crowded conditions, some people still choose a life of hunting and fishing. One of the greatest hunting books is D. Brian Plummer's *Tales of a Rat Hunting Man*, in which the author pursues rodents across British wastelands, at one point hunting rats in a giraffe carcass at a livestock disposal facility. In his book *The Way of the Hunter*, Thomas McIntyre writes, "In the last bomb-cratered city, someone will fly a bird of prey over the wreckage, or turn his dog out after game in the vacant lots among the rubble."

And maybe: cast a bait into a sewage ditch, hoping for minnows.

A distant future? Perhaps not. There are signs the American sporting landscape is already becoming limited for the everyday hunter and angler. Public lands remain the sole reason hunting and fishing are available for the masses. Most prime sporting ground is rapidly being tied up in expensive leases. Blue-ribbon trout waters once considered navigable and open to public use now command fees of $500 or more a day. Barbed wire is strung across streams from Pennsylvania to Montana. I grew up in a time when unposted meant open to the public. Now those places are ringed with No Trespassing signs.

But people will catch fish wherever there are fish. Fly fishing for carp has become fashionable. Carp are certainly fine game fish (despite being non-native), but one wonders if the rise in carp fishing correlates to a decline in trout fishing opportunity. A group of anglers recently gained internet notoriety for fishing (successfully) down storm drains. Is that merely a stunt, or is it because the local ponds are now guarded closely by homeowners' associations?

When it comes to microfishing, the smaller finned species can live just about anywhere . . . in city park ponds, in narrow drainage ditches, in canals, in the overlooked little seeps and creeks. A microfishing kit can be stowed in the smallest apartment. As long as there's water, you will be able to go microfishing.

But microfishing in the United States isn't borne of necessity, not yet. Despite the growth of expensive leases and private fishing clubs, there's still plenty of free opportunity available, from city fishing piers to wilderness areas. No, for now, microfishing here traces its genesis to another popular angling trend: life listing.

My introduction to both life listing and microfishing originated when an Illinois resident named Ben Cantrell wrote me in response to a blog I had written on sucker fishing. He regularly fished a local spot he dubbed "Garvana" due to its large congregations of shortnose gar. Would I be interested in checking it out?

He didn't have to ask twice. I met him on a warm summer morning, and we bushwhacked into a surprisingly remote Central Illinois river. The river ran a bit high and muddy, and after thirty minutes of fishing we had not located any gar. I felt no concern; in my fishing life I've spent plenty of fishless hours and days. Indeed, I did not catch many of the fish I focused on in this book until the last hour or even last minutes of a trip. That's fishing.

Not so for Ben. He immediately shifted tactics. There was nearly always some fish that would be biting. The thought of spending a couple of hours in fruitless quest for a gar seemed like a waste of a good opportunity, especially if there was a chance of new species.

Ben is a fishing life lister, one who keeps track of the species he catches on hook and line. This concept is well known among birders, who meticulously track the species they see. A lot of anglers are goal-oriented: they have lists of destinations they'd like to visit and trophy fish they'd like to catch. Some participate in quests like the Cutthroat Slam. But the concept of specifically seeing how many species you catch is just beginning to take off. A small group of enthusiasts—most of them know each other—plan trips for knuckle-sized darters, human-sized sharks, and everything in between. They share their photos and trip reports on blogs and social media, and record their lists on websites like Roughfish.com and Species Hunters.

Ben fished a bit when he was growing up, but it remained a casual sport, at best, until he attended the University of Wisconsin as a graduate student. Surrounded by lakes and world-class fishing, he started going out more. But focusing on walleyes every trip didn't fit his personality.

"I admit it. I'm obsessive by nature," Cantrell says. "I think it runs in my family. When I get into a hobby, I get really into it."

He always loved keeping records, which led him to a career in engineering with Caterpillar. In college, he was a competitive power lifter—a sport demanding a detailed and precise training regime.

That dedication to detail fueled his hobbies, too. "At one point, my big hobby was craft beer," he says. "I kept track of every kind of beer I'd ever had. My list grew to 1,500. Then I started fishing."

He began noting the species he caught. When he stumbled upon the Roughfish website in 2010, he was—pardon the pun—hooked. That site had a feature that allowed members to list their species caught and contains detailed information on catching just about anything you could imagine.

"I suddenly realized all the fish I could be catching," he says. "I don't keep track of beer any more. I only have room for one obsession in my life."

I felt intrigued by this focus. When I met him in Illinois, his list was nearly three hundred species. How could he rack up such numbers? He planned trips with the precision of military operations, listing all potential "targets" and developing plans to catch them. It also meant he never lingered very long, as time spent in futile casting was time that could be spent adding new species to the list. Steelhead fishing, where you might spend a week before getting a solid hit, would be Ben's idea of a medieval torture chamber.

As we switched our focus from gar to other fish on that Illinois river, it became apparent that most of the larger species were not biting. He began rigging up tiny hooks on his ultralight rods. So tiny, I could barely see them. I soon learned an essential truth of life listing: most fish species are really, really small.

I saw a swirl of tiny silvery fish circling in front of us. Ben had said we were going to be microfishing, but I wasn't quite prepared for how "micro" he meant.

"Are you really going to try to catch those little fish?" I asked.

"I've caught fish a lot smaller than that," Cantrell said.

Cantrell demonstrated his technique. He put a tiny dab of worm on the hook and dangled the line right into the school of minnows. He stood perfectly still, intent on watching the darting forms below him. Then he jerked the rod in a swift motion, bringing up a small sand shiner.

"When a fish strikes, you have to pop the rod," he said. "The pop is the key."

He handed me his rod. I concentrated on the minnows, many of them too small to even be considered bait. I had my first taste of the total concentration required by microfishing. Nothing but me and minnows. I also had the vague sense I was losing my mind.

I saw a minnow nip at the hook. I pulled back and missed it. Another minnow swirled. I set the hook. Nothing.

"Your pop is terrible," Cantrell said.

I kept at it. Microfishing involves sight fishing—you have to see the small fish to get the bait right in front of them—and the fish nearly always have an interest in the bait. Catching them, even with the tiny Japanese hooks made especially for this task, is another matter.

After a dozen failed attempts, I lifted the rod—and there was my sand shiner, an admittedly nondescript pale minnow.

"Your pop is still terrible," Cantrell said. "But you got a new lifer."

A new lifer. I immediately felt a new dimension opening up in my fishing life. After I went home, I began researching the growth of life listing, and the same names kept popping up, anglers who embarked on month-long species catching road trips and one guy who had caught more than one thousand species, including tilapia out of mall fountains. I wanted to meet them. It turns out, I didn't have to look far. They came to me.

❧

Life list anglers spend a lot of time researching locations for obscure and difficult-to-catch species. They trade spots with each other. There becomes a bit of a circuit for certain fish: if you want to catch a walking catfish, for instance, there's a section of canal in Big Cypress National Preserve that everyone visits.

Quite by accident, my local creek fishing spot may be the world's greatest chiselmouth fishery. This is a decidedly modest claim. I have yet to meet an Idaho angler who even knows what a chiselmouth is.

This is not a microfish. In the stream I fish, many reach a foot or more. Their namesake feature is indeed a chisel on its mouth, a flat hard edge that forms the bottom lip. When spawning, their silvery sides contain bright-orange highlights. I'm partial to them.

One summer day, I caught some particularly nice ones after an evening of fishing. I couldn't really share my success with my neighbors, so I did what modern anglers do: posted a photo on a life list fishing social media site.

Within minutes, someone with the unlikely name of Greenwood Vytautus Champ posted a comment: "Sexy." Seconds later, my phone dinged again, this time a private message from the same person.

"Hey Dude!" it began. "Me and my buddy Alex are heading out West and we're wondering if you could help us with finding chiselmouths."

About ten minutes later I received a message from someone named Alex Orr. "Hey, I'm in a species fishing contest and would love to find chiselmouth. Would be willing to trade you spots for fish you want to catch."

I wrote back that I'd be happy to take them to my chiselmouth spot. They told me to expect them in two weeks or so.

Alex and Greenwood keep life lists, but they were participating in a particular variation of listing: the Roughfish June Species Contest. Every June, the site offers a custom fishing rod to the angler who records the most freshwater, standard-sized species (in one of the rifts of the life listing community, the site's owners have a bit of antagonism about microfishing).

The contest began as a way for versatile anglers to show their chops around their local waters. Alex decided that wasn't enough. A contractor, he began taking the month of June off, and fishing across the country, in a whirlwind characterized by road food, late-night campouts and sleep deprivation. He had won the contest three straight years, piling up progressively larger lists of fish. The year he contacted me, he headed west from his Minnesota home—an unusual route given that species diversity tends to increase as you head south.

In his photos on social media and fishing forums, Alex almost always appears shirtless, a large Darth Vader tattooed across his chest. His earlobes are pierced with cylindrical gauges, and a cigarette usually dangles from his mouth.

While Alex is tall and thin, Greenwood bears a superficial resemblance to *School of Rock* vintage Jack Black. While he only recently completed his GED, he's known in the rough fish circles for his encyclopedic knowledge of fish. As I was soon to discover, very few PhD fisheries researchers possess the depth and breadth of Greenwood's taxonomic knowledge. He takes a similar obsessive approach to death metal; his entire wardrobe consists of black t-shirts bearing the insignia of bands like Gorgon and Decapitated Cattle.

I began following their current road trip via Roughfish.com, as the site posts a leaderboard with latest contest entries. They quickly ticked off the expected species around their Minnesota home, then began picturing more exotic fishes as they headed west: rudd from Iowa, Jack Dempsey cichlid in South Dakota, grayling in Montana, Utah sucker in Utah, Mozambique tilapia in Idaho. They were getting closer.

I got a phone call a couple days later. I made arrangements to meet them in a nearby parking lot; they arrived in a low-slung white van, seemingly every inch occupied by fishing rods, tackle, and snacks. They hopped out of the car and made friendly introductions, but it was clear they were on a mission. We drove about twenty-five minutes to my spot, the contest anglers following me as Boise's high desert foothills shifted into the ponderosa pine forests of the Rockies. As signs of the city faded, a mid-sized river flowed along the increasingly winding road. We parked in a little turn off.

"Where the hell are we?" Alex asked. "This is a rad area."

He looked around appreciatively, then rigged up and sprinted down the bank. Greenwood followed, both eager to hook a chiselmouth, a species they'd never caught.

"What would you say our chances are?" Greenwood asked.

I hesitated. This is always a risky question. "I catch them nearly every time I come here."

I directed Alex to fish a little pool below a rock, where the chiselmouth often hold. Greenwood fished a little riffle slightly downstream. A fish swiped at his worm. "That looked like a small-mouth," he said.

"There aren't smallmouth in here," I replied.

Of course, on the next cast Greenwood landed a smallmouth bass. I saw him glance at Alex, and I saw the doubt enter his eyes. I could feel the unspoken question hanging in the air: Did we just follow this guy to a fishing dead end?

Taking someone fishing to a special spot always gives me butterflies, especially if the fishing is a "sure thing." Because fishing is never a sure thing, not really. I've been in the opposite situation so many times, where someone guarantees great fishing and it turns out to be a skunk.

Twenty minutes later, the bass remained the only fish caught. Usually, chiselmouth bite as soon as the bait drifts by them. I fidgeted. Greenwood asked me if I had ever caught the Wood River bridgelip sucker. I had not. He informed me that it was a subspecies so distinct that many biologists considered it a separate species. I felt in over my head. I began to apologize for the lack of fish, but Alex appeared more understanding. (As I've gotten to know him since, I've found that the Darth Vader tattoo and often

angry social media posts mask someone unfailingly kind and generous, one of those people who actually *would* give you the shirt off
his back. If he was wearing a shirt.)

Twenty minutes in chiselmouth fishing felt like an hour. Then
Alex's rod made a light tick, and he hoisted a small 4-inch fish
onto the bank. We looked at the square jaw, the defining feature
of this minnow.

"Yeah, boy," Alex said, trembling slightly. "I can't believe this."

"It's a small one," I offered.

"It's a chiselmouth," he replied.

He cast out again, and this time his rod bounced harder, and
soon he had a proper chiselmouth, about 10 inches and its sides
streaked red in breeding coloration. Now Alex sat down on the
bank to compose himself.

After a photo, in which he appears to be bowing down and
worshiping the fish, he released it and hand rolled a cigarette. "Any
fish you want to catch, I'll tell you the spot," he said. "You can have
anything. Dude, anything."

Greenwood added, "We have a thing for big minnows."

I like chiselmouths. They are a cool-looking, overlooked fish.
But I hadn't quite expected this response, and said so.

"Dude, look at me," Alex said. "Does it look like much has
gone right in my life?"

He went on to win the contest with sixty-eight species caught
that June, more than many anglers will catch in a lifetime.

After the chiselmouth success, I began getting more inquiries
from the avid species hunters. One of those requests was from
Steve Wozniak. Because I had been spending way too much time
on life listing websites, I knew he was not the Apple guy. In species
fishing circles, though, he had achieved the same legendary status.
He was inarguably the life lister with the highest species count, a
whopping 1,767 at the time of this writing. A gregarious business
executive, he writes a blog, *1000 Fish*, that recounts his trips in

stories filled with not only fish but also accounts of bad roads, bad food, a colorful cast of supporting characters, self-effacing humor, and endless fish puns.

Wozniak began this quest in the fall of 1988, when he and a buddy returned from a day of bat ray fishing near his California home. "The question came up over dinner as to who had caught the most species of fish," he says. "I am scary, unhealthy competitive. I added them up and came up with sixty or seventy species. I won and I was very happy with this."

As he drove home, he kept thinking of other species. As an inveterate list maker, an idea began to form in his head. "What happened next is a combination of male psychology and my own deviant personal psychology," he says.

He began with a lifetime goal to catch one thousand species. He travels a lot for work, allowing him to often add a few days or hours of fishing wherever he goes. He started adding species quickly, and in 2007, he reached his goal.

"I was sitting on this boat off the coast of Norway," he says. "I honestly didn't know what would happen. It was like my high school hockey team, when we won the state championship. We had put so much time into that, and then we achieved it. I got home and I just kept thinking 'What's next?' I wondered with fishing, with my goal met, if I was now going to have to take up golf."

He sat in the boat, reflecting, and then the captain pointed to a school of fish below. "I grabbed a rod and was right back in it," he says. "It was on to two thousand. I *think* I can get there. It's not going to be easy."

As with any obscure subculture, life list fishing has its internal rifts and petty feuds, its purists and rogues. Nearly all life list anglers detest bowfishing, and species caught by means other than hook and line don't count. Some, like Alex, have even more stringent standards: he considers fishing guides and lodges, for instance, a form of cheating.

Wozniak can be a polarizing figure. Some complain about his use of guides, his willingness to fish in pay ponds, even his potty humor on the blog. However, I've also noticed this: I've never met one of his detractors who has actually fished with him, or even met him.

Wozniak takes it in stride. In fact, he even seems to egg it on through his celebration of fishing spots that are unconventional, to put it mildly. He has bribed security guards to fish mall fountains. He once visited a backyard pond in Switzerland to catch sculpin that the owners were keeping there for trout bait. One blog recounts a "fee fishing area" in Japan, where he caught two trout species after the owners dumped the fish in a bathtub-sized pool in front of him. When he got criticized for that, he took a trip to a fish hatchery and caught a fish in one of the holding tanks.

This drives certain anglers stark raving mad, but I suspect that he's just trolling those who take this too seriously. Yes, Wozniak has a long list of world records (those records, he points out, are in part due to his extensive time spent fishing, and in part because many species listed by the International Game Fish Association are so obscure they didn't even have submissions until he entered). And yes, he's competitive. But he also is clearly having fun and not afraid to show the silly side of this quest.

Those who *have* fished with him describe him universally as friendly and funny, and a gracious guest, as I found out for myself when he visited me in Boise on his chiselmouth quest. Accompanying him was Martini Arestogui, himself a notable figure in the angling community. His father, Marty, holds the record for the number of world-record fish, and has compiled a lengthy list of fishing firsts. Martini, now a graduate student in fisheries at the University of Washington, has his own lengthy list of world records as well as a life list numbering hundreds of species.

He frequently joins Steve on his road trips and plays a bit of the straight man. They showed up at my door early on an unseasonably cool summer morning. I felt considerably less optimistic about our chances. The winter had brought record snowfall, and that snow now melted into the streams, making them high and muddy. I had yet to catch any chiselmouths, or any other fish.

Steve and Martini knew the routine and seemed to accept it. They surveyed the roiling water in front of us; they both fished enough that they knew this wasn't going to be easy. They rigged up, and while both will take guided trips, they are elite anglers, and it quickly showed as both caught largescale suckers within minutes. Martini added a Columbia sculpin, a species I had never caught here and one that also was missing from Steve's life list. Steve suggested if Martini kept this up, he'd be thrown into the raging stream.

The chiselmouths didn't show. I finally had to leave for work, but they stayed at it until sundown. Martini caught his first mountain whitefish, and they caught an impressive number of suckers, as well as rainbow trout and northern pikeminnows. But no chiselmouths. They took it in stride and took off across Idaho in pursuit of other new species. They returned to Boise two days later. They spent more hours at my spot and each caught chiselmouths. Martini's was a world record.

Most anglers will never have the stamina, interest, or resources to pull off hard-core life listing. But maybe, as with birding, listing can inspire everyday fishermen to learn more about what is in their local waters. Life listers have already contributed to scientific knowledge, documenting species in streams outside their known range, and recording the spread of invasives. Apps like iNaturalist, used by anglers, offer another way to contribute to what researchers call citizen science. But maybe it's a mistake to attach too much meaning to either microfishing or life listing. It's best to keep the pursuit of shiners, or chiselmouths, light-hearted—a humorous antidote to a time in history when it's all too easy to take things too seriously.

As Steve Wozniak puts it, "There is something profoundly funny about a 250-pound man standing in a stream trying hard to catch something the size of his pinky toe. If you can't laugh at yourself for this, you really can't laugh at anything."

Chapter Eleven

What Happens in Miami

I stood on the bow of the boat, sweating in the humidity as we drifted. A movement in the air caught my eye, as a red-shouldered hawk glided just over my head. I followed it as it lifted its talons, plummeting to the ground. I could make out something thrashing; the hawk had clearly scored a meal. As it lifted off, I saw the clear form of a very large and very-much-still-alive green iguana, a Central and South American lizard.

The hawk again flew over the boat with its prey. Around me, Egyptian geese—a common African waterfowl species—began squawking on high alert, even though the hawk would be occupied for some time.

The raptor drifted out of sight. I raised my fly rod and laid out another cast, twitching my streamer through the water. I located my target holding tight against a submerged clump of vegetation. Peacock bass, the premiere sport fish of the Amazon River Basin. The fish didn't budge.

I prepared another cast, when several bright-orange Midas cichlids, of Central American origin, drifted past. I contemplated a cast to them, when someone speaking broke my concentration. A friendly man stood by his grill on shore, asking if I had any luck. Another iguana patrolled a few feet away.

Welcome to Miami.

I first fished for peacock bass in Brazil, where many global anglers travel to hook this hard-striking, hard-fighting species. For me, the fishing was an afterthought, as the main point of the trip was to spot jaguars and other mammals in the wild (which I did). My wife and I had a free day, and I noticed an outfitter on a nearby reservoir advertised peacock bass fishing. I signed up.

"Do locals fish here much?" my wife, Jennifer, asked, as we pulled into the boat launch.

Our guide, whose English was only slightly better than our Portuguese, misunderstood, and replied with a laugh, "Yes, it is certainly loco to try to fish here."

Pro-tip: It's a bad sign when your guide tells you you're crazy for fishing in a spot he is taking you. A very bad sign.

I've long ago learned that the guide is usually right, and in this case, he most definitely was. We boated for a few minutes to the middle of the lake. The guide and boat driver shrugged at each other, and we began casting into featureless water. Within minutes, it became clear that not only did the guides not really know much about fishing, they also were quite open about this lack of knowledge. They repeatedly said we would not catch anything. We did not.

I later learned that peacock bass were not actually native to this reservoir, being far from the Amazon Basin. They were introduced there to provide a sport fishery. By most accounts, the peacocks never really prospered.

The same cannot be said for Miami, where in 1984 the Florida Fish and Wildlife Commission intentionally released butterfly peacock bass, reportedly to control non-native tilapia that were proliferating in canals. The fact that peacock bass were legendary sport fish no doubt played a significant role in the decision. Peacock bass are actually cichlids, not bass, with a distinctive yellowish hue and varied spotting patterns, including a spot that looks like a bullseye near the tail.

After the failed fishing attempt in Brazil, I came to South Florida, meeting guide Mark Hall in a city park on a warm

October morning. Hall's parents moved to Florida when he was a young boy, and he spent high school motoring around the canals in his boat, fishing wherever and whenever he could. Within a few minutes, I could tell he was one of the most knowledgeable guides I'd met, but without a hint of an attitude.

He picked up a fly rod and cast, showing me a particular twitching retrieve that mimicked a wounded baitfish; he said it drove peacocks crazy. No sooner had he made this claim than his rod bent over. "Aww, man, I am so, so sorry," he said. "Horrible form. I don't fish with clients. Just wanted to show you this."

I wasn't annoyed or worried, and instead saw this as a good sign. The fish were biting; now it was just up to me. But Hall kept apologizing for the next five minutes, when I landed my own small peacock bass. Three casts later, I landed a much more solid fish.

Peacock bass strike with a fury. Smaller fish fight remarkably like smallmouth bass, while bigger ones seem to go deep and hold fast. I loved all of it.

The fishing was inconsistent on this day. Sometimes I'd see a fish, and put a streamer over it, two, three, five times. And then the fish would slowly drift away. Other times, I'd cast and the peacock would immediately hammer the fly, shaking its head upon the strike as if to dismember the prey.

The exotic nature of the fish was matched by the utter strangeness of where I was fishing. And not strange in the way of, say, a Brazilian river—where you might see a toucan or a jaguar around the bend. That gets your attention, but it all fits together. On a Miami canal, there's the feeling that you don't know exactly where the hell you are.

We'd duck under a thick patch of foliage, and if that was the only context you had, you'd swear you were in the middle of the jungle. But seconds later you'd emerge to a straight canal lined with backyard porches and swimming pools. The canals wound through parks filled with kids playing soccer, vacant lots where iguanas sulked, and sprawling areas lined with the backsides of retail stores. Families paddled by in kayaks. A couple of teenage boys, wearing coveralls, drove by in a johnboat, just two country kids looking for fish. For being surrounded by a city known for its nightlife and ostentatious lifestyles, it was quiet and peaceful. And, dare I say it? Wild.

Casting to those hard-fighting fish, watching hawks with iguanas and a parade of other exotic critters, I could clearly understand the concept of the novel ecosystem. This is an idea that's been promoted a lot lately by some prominent conservationists. They argue that new ecosystems are popping up in a human-created world, and it's unrealistic to expect these new habitats will contain the same mix of species of previous, "pristine" environments. To some, invasive species are not a blight but evolution in action. They say that the entire concept of invasive species is flawed, as species have always moved around the globe, and always will. What's happening in Miami is the wild finding a way to exist.

And I can almost go along with this line of thinking. Reeling in a big peacock bass showing off its bright Amazon color patterns, I might be tempted to groove out on novel ecosystems. There's just one big problem.

What happens in Miami does not stay in Miami.

The stocking of non-native game fish has been a recurring theme in this book. While species like rainbow trout and smallmouth bass have had a disproportionate impact on North American freshwater fish and fishing, intentional sport fish introduction is only one aspect of the invasive species story. In an era of globalization and rapid travel—when people and products move across the planet with speed and ease—species get deposited in new lands in a variety of ways. Often, the introductions are unintentional. Most species actually fail to take hold in their new environment, as the climate or habitat conditions prove far too hostile. Other species find habitats similar to home, but lacking predators and other limiting factors. In these situations, their populations can explode and devastate native species, not to mention agriculture and even human health.

Miami is a global hub of travel and commerce, and a port of entry for people and cargo going to and coming from South America. That cargo includes wildlife, much of it legally imported for the pet trade. Additionally, Miami's well-known warm and sunny climate is amenable to many subtropical and tropical species. And not far outside the city limits is a national park and wilderness in the form of the Everglades. Endless habitat. This adds up to a recipe for invasive species disaster.

The case of Burmese pythons is widely known and reported, perhaps the favorite invasive species story of the mainstream media. These large snakes, escapees or intentionally released pets, have been eating their way through many of the small mammals, wading birds, and reptiles of the Everglades for several years. Images of the pythons wrapped around alligators circulate the internet. A 15-foot snake makes a terrifying villain, one that gets the attention of just about everyone.

But it's just one non-native species in the Everglades. Most people don't look underwater. If they could, they'd see a startling, otherworldly realm of fish from Asia, Africa, and South America. The peacock bass is actually an outlier here because it was intentionally stocked by a state wildlife agency. Most of the non-native fish swimming in the Everglades got here by a less-designed approach: namely, someone dumped out his aquarium pets.

"People believe they're doing their tropical fish a favor by not killing them," says William Loftus, who worked as a fish ecologist in Everglades National Park for thirty-two years. "They turn them loose in a Miami canal, but if those fish start breeding, they don't stay in Miami. Within three years they could be in Everglades National Park."

That's because the interconnecting canal systems extend well outside Miami city limits. These canals were originally built for flood control and agricultural purposes. Water pulsed into the Everglades but also washed away peoples' homes. The canals have a number of destructive environmental impacts: they deliver unfiltered water, heavy in pollutants and fertilizers, straight into Florida's productive bays and estuaries. Conservationists are working to install wetlands and ponds that allow the pollutants to settle out, a difficult but fixable task.

The canals also serve as a non-native fish superhighway system. The Tamiami Canal rings Everglades National Park, creating easy passage from Miami. Loftus has even published a paper suggesting that Everglades water-management regimes, including how canals deliver water to the wetlands, have made the environment even more conducive to non-native fish. Those canals also provide a refuge when the Everglades dries, as it does every year. The only limiting factor to the fish's spread, Loftus says, is the periodic cold snaps that hit the area. After frigid weather, he has found walking catfish, a non-native species from Asia, floating dead in large numbers.

"You will see others that survived the cold, but they often have ulcers from bacteria," he says. "They're infected because the cold suppressed their immune system."

Even in such conditions, some non-native fish do survive, and Loftus says they can return to previous population levels in a few years. "Of course, this might just be selecting for fish that are more resistant to the cold," he says with a grim laugh.

The canals also make surviving the cold easier, as they are fed by groundwater that keeps them at a constant temperature. This has made the park a veritable sanctuary for non-native fish. In the 1970s, only two non-native fish lived in the Everglades. That number increased to fifteen established non-native species by 2015, and continues to grow. Loftus also notes that the number and frequency of cold spells are decreasing, likely due to climate change—creating even more favorable conditions for non-native fish.

How are these fish affecting the Everglades? Loftus says that, right now, it's almost impossible to answer. "We just don't know for most species in the wild," he says. "There is very little funding to study impacts. It is very difficult to determine impacts in a complex system like the Everglades, especially without funding."

Studying invasive species is often a challenge, as the invasions often occur in environments already changed substantially by people. Cane toads, for instance, are a notorious invasive species in Australia, accused of devastating native and beloved wildlife. Rick Shine, an Australian snake researcher, decided to undertake a comprehensive evaluation of cane toad impacts when the species showed up in his study area. What he found surprised him. Some native animals were indeed nearly wiped out by the toads. But other species were already in decline due to a variety of factors, and the toad became a convenient scapegoat. As he tells in his marvelous book *Cane Toad Wars*, the real picture was much more complex than anyone realized, but that actually made finding solutions easier.

The Everglades is dealing with a host of issues, including water supply and water pollution in a state growing and developing at a mind-boggling rate. It can be difficult to determine what is having the most impact on the environment. But Loftus and other researchers have shown, in a laboratory setting, that some non-native fish can negatively impact smaller native fish species. As non-native fish populations grow, he wonders what changes could ripple through the ecosystem. Wading birds, for instance, rely on fish. What if the invaders are not species they will eat?

There is so much still to learn about these fish, but one thing is almost certain: once they're in the Everglades, they're not going away. "The fish get into 1.5 million acres of habitat," Loftus says. "We have nothing in the toolbox to control these things once they're in the environment."

Many agencies and individuals, including Loftus, advocate for education, but, as he says, "It just takes one person dumping an aquarium to introduce a new species, and what are the chances they'll get caught?"

There is perhaps no instance where the old cliché about an "ounce of prevention" rings so true. Some species could potentially wreak extreme havoc, the equivalent of underwater pythons. Loftus and other fisheries biologists are currently conducting a risk assessment to determine what fish pose the biggest threats.

"Right now, there are prohibited fish, but they often get put on the list after they've already become established and start doing damage," Loftus says. "By that time, the cat is already out of the bag. We need to determine which species should be legal in the tropical fish hobby and which species should be prohibited."

Managers have their work cut out for them. You prevent one invasion, but there's always more fish sitting in shipping containers, swimming in home aquaria, breeding in a tropical fish farm. Waiting for a hurricane, for a flood, for someone to get bored of their pets. Waiting, waiting.

I drove out of Miami into the Everglades along the Tamiami Canal, gritting my teeth through bumper-to-bumper traffic and passing the usual assortment of big-box stores, tract homes, and chain restaurants. And then, almost like crossing a line in the sand, it all gave way to swaying grass and water and billboards for airboat rides. I saw alligators drifting like logs.

I wanted to catch some of the exotics that swam these waters. I figured that having some worms might up my chances, so I stopped in a little gas station.

"We don't carry worms," said the attendant. "'Bout the only place that does is the Skunk Ape Center."

Skunk Ape Center? This sounded too good to be true, so I drove out of the national park to the Big Cypress National Preserve. Sure enough, I saw a sign for a campground, safari tours, and the promised skunk ape research center. I pulled in. The research into the Everglades' man-ape seemed to largely involve selling copious amounts of souvenirs associated with the beast. I looked through the various fuzzy photos interspersed with knick-knacks, when a burly man appeared. I asked about getting some worms.

"They all died," he said. "You looking to fish for oscars and cichlids?"

"Yeah," I said.

"Use hot dogs," he said. "It's the best bait for 'em. An oscar will just hammer a hot dog."

I asked him if he suggested any spots, and he replied, "They're thick in here. Just find a pull-off along the canal and cast by a stump. They'll find you."

I parked at the first pull-off and peered into the water. Sure enough, the water swarmed with fish. I immediately recognized a peacock bass darting away. While they were stocked in Miami under the promise that they wouldn't spread outside the city, they had penetrated well into the Everglades. They also proved to have limited value in controlling non-native tilapia, gulping whatever fish came their way. I also immediately noticed Florida gar, a native species and of course one of my favorites, cruising through the water.

I rigged up my hook, sheepishly adding a hot dog. As it wasn't cooked, it barely stayed on. As soon as it hit the water, a swirling school of fish attacked—reminding me of certain fish-feeding attractions at large aquariums. I reeled in a spotted sunfish, a native species. I cast again, this time closer to a tangle of submerged tree roots. Again a frenzy erupted, and I soon had on another fish. This one had bright stripes and neon highlights, a Central American species known as a Mayan cichlid. A popular local name is atomic sunfish, which given their bright colors, stocky shape and voracious appetite, seems perfectly appropriate.

With my third cast I hooked another cichlid, and as I reeled it in I noticed a log moving. Fast. Just as my mind pieced together this puzzle, the "log" launched and opened its jaws wide, snapping at my fish. Alligator. Heart in my throat, I reeled frantically as the alligator lunged for the fish. I landed it, but barely. The alligator waited just below me. I decided to move on.

I drove a short distance and parked again in a thick clump of trees. While the canal looked channelized, everything else about the scene appeared like a primeval jungle. Egrets and herons flew through the trees. Schools of fish swam through the water. I saw an otter jump off a bank.

I wasted no time in casting and again immediately attracted a swirl of ravenous fish. A pattern emerged. I'd catch a mix of spotted sunfish and Mayan cichlids, but after a few thrashing fish, an alligator or two would show up and chomp at my catch. One look at their gaping jaws proved quite effective at keeping me moving.

I reached an area where a narrow pipe backed up a canal channel into a large pond. Some stumps lined one side and I cast a Mepps spinner hard against it. I feared a snag but within two turns of the reel, I saw a fish dart out and savagely strike it. It wasn't large, but it bent my ultralight and fought with pulsing runs. As I got it closer, I saw a bright spot on its tail, and a dark, solid form. An oscar. This common and pugnacious pet store purchase now swims the Everglades. This one was as big as my outstretched hand.

I continued this tactic as I moved along the canal system, and I was rewarded with plenty of nice oscars. I also spotted some exotic species I hadn't caught: plate-sized blue tilapia often floated on the outskirts of the feeding frenzies, and periodically I'd see a pleco catfish clinging to rocks. But they showed no interest in my baits. I decided I had enough of the exotics. The next Mayan cichlid I caught, I bonked it on the head and cut it into strips. I cast out and soon had a gar on the line, giving my ultralight a thrashing fight. The fish almost broke me off on tree roots, twice, but I landed it. And as I looked at the elongated snout of the gar, it gave me hope. The gar had been swimming around since the time of the dinosaurs. Somehow I doubt a few of these non-native interlopers would interfere much with it. Native fish would swim on.

The next day, I stopped at a place I've since come to call Gartopia given its huge schools of this favorite fish. An impounded canal, it is one of those waters where you can realistically expect to catch a fish every single cast. And I did: not only Florida gar but largemouth bass, spotted sunfish, channel catfish, brown bullhead, bluegill, warmouth, Mayan cichlid, and oscar. A mix of natives and exotics. (And I could have caught species most consider "saltwater" fish. Snook and tarpon tolerate a wide range of salinity levels, and can be caught in these same canals.)

Soon, I had caught more than enough fish for the trip that my attention began to wander. I watched birds, tried new lures, thought about where I'd have a nice dinner. And then, a bowfin appeared. Just 6 feet from where I stood, the prehistoric fish settled in shallow water and silently waited for prey. Another native, supremely adapted to this place.

My calm afternoon crumbled. Just when I was about to award myself Master Angler status, the bowfin showed up, sure to make me look like a rank amateur. This is a fish for panic attacks. If you've never seen one, the bowfin bears a loose resemblance to an eel that competes in body-building competitions. With a thick head and stout tail, it looks primitive, and it is: this is a fish that has been hunting rivers and wetlands for hundreds of millions of years. While others call it mudfish, dogfish, or even cypress trout, it would be more accurate to simply nickname it badass.

I came unglued at the sight of the fish, devising a strategy in my head. I grabbed my flimsy travel rod and quickly walked to the other side of the pond. I cast a redworm into a pod of spotted sunfish, and landed one immediately. I unceremoniously thumped it on the head, and cut a bloody chunk of meat off. I rigged up my heavier rod.

The bowfin remained, seemingly in ambush mode. I rushed, my fingers trembling as I tied on a large hook. I checked my drag, hooked the bait, and tossed it a couple of feet from the bowfin. In seconds, it swam over, paused and looked at this strange meal that had dropped from above.

The fish opened its mouth. For a second, the motion seemed so subtle, I wondered if it actually had taken the bait. It began swimming away, and I couldn't see the sunfish. I pulled back on the rod. The water exploded.

A bowfin feels like you've hooked a jackhammer. Many game fish make powerful runs, leap in the air, and shake their head. The bowfin thrashes. It's electric. My angling self-image evaporated as I tried to control the explosion. The fish took drag. I started steering it towards shore. It instead surged towards the rusted metal of the drainage pipe. I attempted to horse it away from this obstacle, but failed. My line snapped.

I sat down. Shaking. Shaken. Fish still do this to me.

Now I wanted to catch nothing but bowfin. I cast out another chunk of sunfish along the vegetation. I caught a Florida gar and lost a monstrous channel catfish—both fish that would have thrilled me any other time—but I couldn't shake bowfin dreams.

And then it reappeared, in the exact same spot. Bowfin, even after being hooked, project an air of profoundly not giving a shit. That may be anthropomorphic, but it's hard to look at the bowfin and not see a bit of an attitude.

I again checked my knots, checked my drag. I ran through my strategy in my head, including a plan to aggressively keep the fish away from the jagged pipe. I baited up my hook, took a deep breath, and cast. The bowfin hesitated. It stared at the bait, hovered near it. And then it gulped. Game on. Again.

The rod doubled and vibrated. I let out a curse, stepped back, and nearly bumped into a guy with a camera. Just as Everglades fish on the line draw alligators, they also often serve as a tourist magnet. I realized that my exclamations and bent rod had drawn a crowd of national park bikers and walkers.

Hemingway wrote, "Somebody just back of you while you are fishing is as bad as someone looking over your shoulder while you write a letter to your girl." Indeed. I didn't care about losing the fish in front of my audience, but I now felt both self-conscious and annoyed.

"What do you have on?" the man standing right next to me asked. "It must be a big one."

"Can't talk," I muttered.

"What did you say? Did you say it's a bass?" he then turned to other tourists. "He thinks it's a bass."

"Bowfin," I mumbled, as the fish made a surge. I had steered it away from the pipe, but now it headed towards a submerged stump.

"Catfish? Could it be a catfish?" someone else asked.

The man repeated the question. "Do you think it's a catfish, or a bass?"

"Bowfin!" I yelled, hoping to end this line of questioning.

"I don't think he knows what it is," the man said.

The fish seemed to tire. I had it along the bank. I tried to remain calm as I swung the bowfin onto the bank. I heard people exclaim and felt aware of others snapping photos. The bowfin rejuvenated and began thrashing. I jumped on top of it and hoisted the catch.

The man next to me took a step back. "It's not a bass; it's just a mudfish," he announced. He began walking away, waving off the other spectators. "It's just a mudfish."

Not this again. Once more, I had run smack into a lack of native fish appreciation. And if people don't care about this awesome, primitive predator—if they can't appreciate the lives of these fish so perfectly at home in these wetland waters—how can we realistically convince them of the threat of invasive species?

I pushed that thought out of my head and reveled in the bowfin. It was time to call it a day. As I drove back towards Miami and my flight home, I stopped in a national park visitor center to purchase a little something for my young son.

I picked out a cute albeit overpriced ranger outfit. As I approached the checkout, the lady said, "That. Is. Expensive. I. Just. Want. To. Make. Sure. You. Can. Afford. That."

I stepped back from her loud and halting speech style, trying to place what accent this was. "It. Is. Thirty. Dollars," she continued.

"Huh?"

"THIRTY. DOLLARS."

She said it without malice, and instead with a voice both kind and condescending. I saw her staring at my shirt. My shirt: splattered with mud, fish slime and guts, blood and bits of sun-baked hot dog. I had been noticing a strange, fishy odor permeating the gift shop, but I now understood it was coming from me. I realized, suddenly, that I must look like I had been living under a bridge for the past few months. She was talking to me slowly and carefully, like I was a man unhinged, someone whose life had fallen badly apart.

"It's fine," I said. "I'm getting this as a souvenir for my son."

I could see her assessing my parenthood potential. "You live nearby?" she asked.

"Idaho," I said.

"Wow. That must be a really big trip. For *you*. You must be proud. So far from home."

She may have slightly misjudged who I was, but I readily admit that it's easy to feel far from home in the Everglades. Just as it's easy to write off the strange and colorful fish swimming there as just another form of Florida wackiness, the kind of thing that might appear in a Carl Hiaasen novel. The arid sagebrush desert and ponderosa pine forests of my Idaho home feel about as far from Florida as you can get. But, as I was soon to discover, Florida is not the only place with weird tropical fish so very far from home.

CHAPTER TWELVE

Convicts in the Hot Springs

Back in Idaho: Our tent rustled in the warm breeze as our son, Derek, moved rocks with his Tonka bulldozer. We sat in our camp chairs, enjoying the view of mountain peaks framing a wide valley. A river burbled in the background. It was the July 4th holiday weekend, and we had the place pretty much to ourselves.

We were in a free, public camping spot on Bureau of Land Management property. Last night, we had noticed a Subaru parked about a half mile away, but otherwise the campground was empty. While the rest of the country enjoyed fireworks and parades, picnics and parties, RV caravans and crowded beaches, we enjoyed pronghorn antelope trotting through the sage.

This remote valley in Central Idaho appeared to have little, if anything, in common with South Florida. In fact, Idaho's entire statewide population contained about a million fewer residents than could be found in Miami-Dade County. The nearest town from our camp, Howe (population 220), sat 45 miles of mostly gravel road away. I suspect most people in the United States would not believe such a place exists.

As my son continued his construction project, I rigged up a couple of rods and strolled through the camp site and across the gravel road. I approached what appeared to be a misplaced farm pond, one barely larger than an Olympic swimming pool. Known as Barney Hot Springs, it was one of the main draws for campers. It was also a highly unusual fishing hole.

I approached the bank and saw swirls of color: large tropical fish circled much of the pond. Some families visited here to feed the fish. I felt relieved none of them were around, as I planned to catch some on hook and line.

I cast a chunk of nightcrawler into the pond and had a hit as soon as the bait sank into the water. I lifted my ultralight and quickly reeled in a fish lined with alternating bars of black and white: a convict cichlid, native to Central America. An escaped convict in the hot springs. I cast out again, and my worm flipped off my hook. This induced a feeding frenzy that drew to mind Hollywood piranhas. A swirl of baby-blue-colored fish circled 10 feet out from where I stood. I pitched another bait into their midst and immediately hooked one. Close inspection revealed stripes on this fish too, and I later learned it was an African cichlid species known as a zebra mbuna. These fish fought over every bait I cast. When Derek tired of his construction projects, I rigged up his Dock Demon rod and soon had him catching cichlids galore.

I switched to a fly rod and a glittery nymph, and cast to some reeds growing along the bank. As I stripped the fly back to me, I felt a savage strike and set the hook. I reeled in a hefty Mozambique tilapia, with large rubbery lips and an almost blackish cast to its body. I caught a few more of these. I saw some smaller fish dart by, including the occasional goldfish. I tried casting smaller baits to them, but the cichlids always beat them to the bait.

You stand in remote mountains and can convince yourself that this place is largely untrammeled by humanity. So it's jarring to find that pond filled with tropical fish. Just like the Everglades.

Unlike the Everglades, the cichlids and tilapia have zero chance of spreading, even though a channel runs out of the pond and eventually connects to the Little Lost River. The Little Lost is cold, and winters bring ice and snow and raging flows . . . conditions that tropical fish find intolerable. They're stuck in the pond and a bit of its outflow. Managers have not paid attention to them. One woman I talked to, who grew up 45 miles away in Howe, said she had been coming to see the fish for fifty years.

Coming across African and Central American fish in remote, wild country seems like a novelty, but it's really not. The fact that tropical fish are not in every US pond, lake, and river is not because most pet owners have restraint. It's because most waters are just too cold. Anywhere in this country where the water temperature is amenable to tropical fish, you can safely bet that the water indeed has tropical fish. Many hot springs actually get *too* hot; far warmer than anything you'd find in an African lake. Barney feels luke-warm; Jennifer loves visiting hot springs but found that Barney was a bit cool for enjoyable soaking. The fact that fish swarmed her feet may not have helped.

Around the Western United States, though, some springs remain a cozy temperature for fish year-round. Springs large and small in Utah, Wyoming, Montana, and other states host a long list of tropical species. They've become favorite dumping grounds for aquarium pets: think *Finding Nemo* meets *Call of the Wild*.

Even some of the most highly protected places in the country are not immune to these introductions. Grand Teton National Park is known for its abundant native fish populations, including Snake River fine-spotted cutthroat trout. But the park's Kelly Warm Springs is home to non-native guppies, green swordtails, madtoms (a small catfish), and even bullfrogs. These species have spread down a warm channel and are now within 10 feet of the Snake River, a refuge for native fish.

While the upper Snake River is almost certainly too cold to support a population of guppies, fisheries managers wisely don't want to take any chances. In 2015, they began soliciting public comments about a proposed plan to eradicate the non-native species from the springs. The proposal called for a variety of removal techniques including treating the pond with rotenone, lethal to fish but not to humans. However, due to budget constraints and shifting priorities, the fish removal has been delayed. The guppies and madtoms still swim in the shadow of the Tetons.

After my initial visit to Barney, my life listing and microfishing friend Ben Cantrell contacted me about a trip there. Ben's fish quest had kicked into overdrive since I spent time with him in Illinois; he had recently taken trips to the Amazon Basin and Mexico where he racked up large numbers of new fish. His life list had swelled to 550 species. He wanted to visit Idaho and catch a number of interesting natives, but he also felt a visit to the hot springs was a must.

It has become a bit of a pilgrimage for the hard-core listers. Alex Orr and Greenwood Vytautus Champ had visited there on their Western tour, as had Steve Wozniak and Martini Arestogui.

But Barney Hot Springs is not really near anything. In a state filled with spring creeks, wilderness rivers, and other waters teeming with trout, many of my local friends couldn't grasp the appeal of a long and dusty drive just to fish what is essentially a glorified tropical aquarium.

"I can see how it's fun for a two-year-old, but I can't get why you'd travel here to fish in a pond," Jennifer told me when I mentioned my itinerary with Ben. "It seems a bit like it's just padding the list. It feels like cheating."

Nonetheless, the listers love warm springs because they yield a lot of exotic and bizarre creatures. To me, it seemed like the epitome of postmodern fishing . . . casting in wilderness pools for house pets gone wild.

Ben arrived and we rather quickly caught a number of cool native species: largescale sucker, chiselmouth, northern pikeminnow, Columbia sculpin, Utah chub. The fishing was good and the weather beautiful, but Ben was not one to linger on a stream no matter how great the prospects. We began the long, bumpy ride to Barney Hot Springs.

We pulled up to the pond and found a woman standing beside her ATV, staring wistfully into the water. I immediately sensed something awry. The usually clear waters looked muddy and roiled; the sides lined with algae blooms. My eyes scanned the waters for the cichlids.

"The water's still dirty," the woman announced as I got closer.

"Seeing any fish?" I asked.

"I haven't seen any," she said. "I don't know where they could be."

I looked around, and for a second wondered if I had turned at the wrong pond. I had not. This was Barney. I couldn't see any fish.

"Something is wrong," I said to Ben. "This pond was swirling with fish the last time I was here."

"It's not time to panic yet," he said, but he sounded unconvincing.

I walked around the pool, searching for fish. A darting orange form caught my eye. "A goldfish," I called out.

"At least we know there are still fish here," Ben said.

We looked closer and saw a large school of goldfish. Nothing else. We cast our lines into the murky depths of the pond, but nothing bit. What was going on?

Eventually we switched to small hooks and cast nubs of nightcrawler into the goldfish school. We soon each popped out several, some brown like miniature carp and some bright orange like the ones you might win at the county fair. I've caught some strange fish, but this felt a bit too much like catching someone's pet.

Another ATV pulled up, a seemingly unusual amount of traffic for this remote location. The older woman jumped off and looked at our rods. "You finding any fish?" she asked.

"Goldfish," I said.

"Well, at least there's something," she said. "At least something survived."

"Survived?"

"This spring we had a flash flood," she said. "It dumped a bunch of icy water into the pond, and all the fish died. I can't believe they're gone."

It's common to say there are never any guarantees in fishing, but Barney always disproved that idea. It was fish in a barrel. Nature has a way of undoing best-made plans. Ben just stared into water. I pondered whether the algae blooms were due to an infusion of dead fish bodies, or because hundreds of fish had suddenly ceased feeding on the vegetation.

A pickup truck pulled up and a man got out, staring at the water. Barney was positively busy today, as if people had come to pay respects to the lost fish.

We eventually resigned ourselves to the long drive out. As we packed up, yet another pickup truck stopped and two young men stepped out and started putting on waders. They assembled minnow traps and readied thermometers. I told Ben we'd be staying a bit longer.

Skyler Smith, an undergraduate student at Brigham Young University-Idaho, introduced himself. He had dreamed of presenting fish research at the American Fisheries Society conference, and knew he'd need something unique. He found that Barney fit the bill, was relatively close to his university, and was also understudied. Last fall, he began surveying the fauna of the springs, capturing species in minnow traps and writing a paper on the assemblage of species. He presented it at the conference.

He planned to continue to look at Barney's fish community through the summer, recording how this miniature, human-made ecosystem functioned. The spring flood provided an intriguing twist to his work.

"I was surprised by how many fish were in here," he said. "I was not expecting this to happen. I'm sure it has happened at some point, but the history of this spring hasn't really been documented. This is the first recorded instance of a fish kill here."

Among the dead fish bodies floating on the surface were not only tilapia and cichlids but also genuine oddities like the long, wavy clown knifefish and the Amazonian pleco catfish. They were not breeding, and people had not reported seeing them, but they were eking out a living in the depths.

The goldfish, he said, could tolerate cooler water and thus survived the flood. "When we were trapping fish in the fall, before the fish kill, we never caught a goldfish," Smith said. "We saw some swimming around, but they never went in the trap. The other fish would beat them to the bait."

This was similar to what I found when fishing. Previously, the goldfish never got the worm. "Now the goldfish already seem to be prospering," Smith said. "We've set traps and now all we catch are goldfish. I suspect they'll take over the pond."

Of course, he acknowledged that someone would eventually probably dump their aquarium into Barney, starting a new population of exotic species. "The fish may be confined to the pond, but we think it still sends a bad message about introducing fish," Smith said. "It gives this idea that introducing fish is harmless. In most places, it's not harmless at all. We don't want people to think that releasing their pet is something they should consider."

Unlike the Everglades, a flood doesn't move fish around; it's the apocalypse. Barney Hot Springs, as such, becomes an embodiment of a concept conservationists call island biogeography. Wildlife living on a large island are more resilient to fires, floods, predators, disease, climate change, and other dramatic changes. The smaller the island, the more likely a random event can wipe a species out. Barney was a human-made "island," but it was ultimately small and vulnerable in the face of the Idaho wilderness.

Ben sat silently in the car as we pulled away, no doubt pondering the lifelist additions he had narrowly missed. "Come back in a few years and I bet you'll be able to catch some weird fish," I said. I had no doubt I'd be right.

To be clear, I agree with Smith, that introducing fish here, or anywhere, sets a bad precedent. I didn't mourn the loss of the cichlids. I also suspected that Barney fans were already plotting ways to restock the pond. The flood may have provided a natural form of invasive control, but it ultimately wouldn't stop human nature. A new community of colorful fish would soon be swimming the seemingly tranquil waters, unnatural additions to the still wild, untamed world surrounding them.

CHAPTER THIRTEEN

A Monumental Eel

As I talked to anglers during my journeys, I heard a lot of childhood fishing stories. These often involved time with parents and grandparents, exploration of local creeks, surprise encounters with huge fish. So many passionate fishers look back on those times with fondness and nostalgia.

The stories of the "old days" along the Potomac River have a different tone. Many remember dire warnings from their parents of what would happen if they got near the river. It seems everyone has a story of falling in, or seeing someone fall in, and rescue personnel rushing to the scene. The emergency crews were not there to prevent drowning but to make sure the person was up to date on their vaccinations.

Some people admit they didn't even think about the river being there: it was out of sight and out of mind, hidden behind industrial buildings. However, it also inspired riots, because a city's drinking water was tainted with lead and other chemicals. President Lyndon B. Johnson called it a "national disgrace." Even Abraham Lincoln purportedly took a carriage out of the city on summer evenings to escape the Potomac's stench.

And now I'm on this river to go fishing. The Potomac River flows through America's capital city, and appropriately enough, its story is *the* quintessential American story of clean water and river conservation. It is a story of hope, of righting past wrongs, of what this country can do when we put our minds to it. But it's also a cautionary tale. This story isn't over yet, not by a long shot.

—◆—

When I emailed Patrick Kerwin for information on fishing the Potomac, he immediately wrote back, offered to show me around for a May weekend, put me up in a spare room in his apartment, and also provide a culinary tour of DC-area ethnic restaurants.

Patrick is a librarian, working in arguably one of the top positions in that profession. He's an archivist for the Library of Congress, where he runs the correspondence section. He's handled letters handwritten by US presidents as well as those of many of this country's best and brightest minds. When I met him, he had just completed cataloging the correspondence of noted astronomer Carl Sagan. Whatever your stereotype of librarian is, Patrick is sure to shatter them. He wears his hair buzzed off, and has tattoos snaking up his arms. When you see him strolling around the city, he'll likely be holding a cigarillo in one hand and a fishing rod in the other.

Life as an archivist requires an organized and analytical approach, and he brings that to his fishing as well. He once was a competition carp angler but in recent years has shifted to trying to catch the diverse species found in the Potomac (and beyond).

Over dinner of spicy beef stew served on the fluffy injera at a local Ethiopian restaurant, Patrick and his friendly wife Lia shared their ideas for the weekend's fishing. We'd start right in the DC metropolitan area, casting swimbaits and Rapalas to see what we'd catch.

The next morning, we followed an armada of tour buses over the bridge to the river, the green lawns and towering monuments of the Capitol Mall looming in front of us. "The tourists get old," Patrick said. "You catch a fish, and you become one of the attractions."

The trail along the river was groomed and well kept, although the bustling activity of the mall—clicking cameras, urban joggers, wayward frisbees—meant that you never quite forgot you were in the city.

As I rigged up, I saw another angler put down his rod and amble over. As I focused on tying the knot, I suddenly startled when that angler's face appeared just a foot away. He stared, so close I could almost feel his breath.

"Hi," I offered.

He said nothing, just watched what lure I was tying on. "I've never fished here before," I said.

He stood silently and waited as I fumbled through my knots, now self-conscious and uncomfortable. As I stepped back to walk to the water, he finally moved, literally brushing against me as he walked away.

I looked at Patrick, who had burst out laughing. "He just wanted to check out what we were using," Patrick said. "He had an unusual method, but I can tell you're not used to that sort of thing. You looked pretty freakin' awkward."

"He was practically standing *on* me."

"Welcome to city fishing."

We headed over to the wall running along this portion of the river, casting out lures for a couple of hours. The river has become a destination for largemouth bass fishing, even hosting professional tournaments. We hoped for something perhaps a bit more exotic, but nothing was hitting. I walked along the bank, watching carp move in the river's shallows. Some litter collected along the bank, and at one point, a huge, bloated dead rat drifted by.

Mostly, though, I could have been on any river. And even though that morning did not yield any fish, it was a bit of a miracle that we were fishing here at all.

⚬⚬⚬

A common bit of environmental lore suggests that it was the Cuyahoga River catching on fire that launched clean water into the public consciousness. The truth is, by the 1960s, many urban waterways were a toxic soup consisting of industrial pollutants, agricultural runoff, and sewage. The Potomac was not on fire, but the city dumped tons of raw sewage directly into its waters. Algae blooms overtook swaths of river. Fish died. People may have tried to ignore the river, but that eventually proved impossible.

"At the end of the day, the Potomac is the source of the water people drink," says Hedrick Belin, executive director of Potomac Conservancy. "When you turn on the tap in the DC metro area, you're drinking Potomac water."

Still, a solution seemed unlikely at the time, in part because the solution to pollution was seen as outside the federal government's purview. As President Eisenhower remarked, "Water pollution is a uniquely local blight. Primary responsibility for solving the problem lies not with the Federal Government but rather must be assumed and exercised, as it has been, by State and local governments."

This sentiment remains at the heart of clean water debate (and, really, all environmental issues) today. And while that thinking certainly has an emotional resonance—"Act local!"—there's a major problem. Water does not recognize our political boundaries. The Potomac begins in West Virginia and forms part of the border with Maryland and Virginia, in addition to flowing through the District of Columbia.

"Maryland couldn't compel Virginia to stop discharging waste, and vice versa," says Belin.

The solution, ultimately, had to be federal, and it came in the form of the 1972 Clean Water Act, a bipartisan piece of legislation that prohibited direct discharge of pollution into waters without permit, and also regulated indirect sources of pollution. It also funded improvements in wastewater treatment and protected wetlands, which are essentially nature's filter system.

"We needed that strong federal leadership," says Belin. "On the Potomac, it provided major upgrades to many wastewater treatment plants. But just as important, it brought science and funding to watershed issues."

That law can only be described as a spectacular success, one that should be celebrated with the same patriotic fervor as successful military campaigns. Far from crippling local efforts, it allowed local conservationists to actually work on fixable problems. One of the most active groups is Potomac Conservancy, which protects river-friendly forests and farmlands through conservation easements, advocates for clean water, and works with county and municipal governments on water ordinances. The organization celebrates an impressive list of successes, but acknowledges those would not have been possible without strong federal legislation.

The river has responded, with wildlife serving as perhaps the strongest evidence. American shad—migratory fish that make a spawning run from the Atlantic up the river—now have robust runs. Bald eagles and ospreys can be viewed from downtown Washington, DC. Even bottlenose dolphins are showing up in the river's tidal basin.

And people no longer shun the river. They celebrate it. Shops and restaurants in places like Georgetown now boast of their river frontage. People run and bike along river paths, and people picnic in parks. In the headwaters, outfitters offer trips for kayaking and fishing. Stores like L.L.Bean, Patagonia, and REI have set up shop to capitalize on the outdoor lifestyle in the big city.

Everything isn't perfect. There are still fish kills on the river. Heavy rains can bring sewage overflows. Agricultural runoff still adds fertilizers and pesticides to the water. But compared to what the river was like fifty years ago? This is one to toast.

Curiously, the Clean Water Act gets scant mention in the outdoor press. This same press will trumpet the conservation achievements of hunters and anglers, including the importance of wildlife regulations and the funding provided by the sale of fishing licenses. But, surely, the Clean Water Act is equally deserving of sportsman adulation. This legislation is arguably one of the biggest reasons we're still fishing today. But I fear anglers aren't the only ones ignoring water quality. We no longer wake up with the threat of rivers on fire, of bass and catfish replaced with turds and toxic chemicals. And that leads to many of us taking clean water for granted.

━ ⌒

When it became apparent we'd catch no fish, Patrick suggested moving to an urban Potomac tributary stream. We drove a few miles, parking by a series of dated apartment buildings. The creek ran between the housing and a busy interstate, a slice of wildness hidden in plain sight. We walked through a patch of trees to a little spillway, and immediately I could see fish of several varieties milling around.

"Pretty cool to have all these fish right here in the city," said Patrick. "Look at all those cars buzzing by. They have no idea what's even here."

Despite the proximity to a sea of humanity and their vehicles, the scene otherwise looked like a postcard of bucolic nature. Trees lined the banks and an osprey drifted overhead. The waters ran surprisingly clear and, if you could block out the rumbling of traffic, you could hear the bubbling of waterfalls and rapids.

This proved an easy fishing spot, and within minutes I had caught smallmouth bass, redbreast sunfish, green sunfish, and banded killifish. Striped mullet, an algae feeder and not inclined to bite, circled around the deeper pools. Patrick suggested we walk a little ways down the river to look for more species but then noticed that all the sunfish bolted. "Look out in the deeper water," he said.

I strained my eyes but could see nothing. Patrick pointed again. Camouflaged against a large rock, I finally saw it. And there, lurking, was my first sighting of a northern snakehead. Elongated and muscular, it resembled a bowfin, but with a more serpentine flair. A notorious non-native species, they are a popular food in Asian markets. They escaped (or were released) into the Potomac in the early 2000s, eliciting widespread panic.

I jumped up the bank and grabbed a heavier rod I had brought just for such a possibility. I had it already rigged with a swimbait, cast out, and began a slow retrieve. The snakehead didn't move. "Too slow," said Patrick. "They strike fast-moving prey."

I cast again, and this time the snakehead simply drifted out of sight, into a deep pool. Patrick cast his line into the pool, but didn't get a strike. I moved to a new spot, and then heard him yell out. With his rod severely bent over and twisted, I knew this wasn't a bass. Soon he hoisted it up onto the rocks: a snakehead.

It was tough to not make the too-obvious comparison to a snake. A formidable snake. It is easy to see why it strikes fear into so many, why its introduction spawned front-page news stories and even horror movies. When it was first discovered, many believed it could undo the entire Potomac ecosystem and perhaps rivers on the East Coast.

"The snakehead became a poster child for the dangers of invasive species," says John Odenkirk, Potomac fisheries biologist for the Virginia Department of Game and Inland Fisheries.

Throughout this book, I've shown the damage that can be done by non-native species across North America. The snakehead certainly makes a fearsome invasive villain, but have the initial fears about its release actually come to pass?

"I want to emphasize I'm not a proponent of the snakehead. I'm not a proponent of any non-native fish," says Odenkirk. "But I do want to disseminate the most accurate information available. The jury is still out, but the snakehead definitely doesn't seem to have the major impact that people believed it would."

Odenkirk notes that a lot of the initial fear centered on its impact on the Potomac's now-popular largemouth bass fishery (and it should be noted, largemouth bass are also non-native to this river). While snakeheads and largemouths do eat many of the same foods, there's no research to suggest snakeheads are decreasing bass numbers. Fish surveys typically result in fifty to one hundred bass per hour of effort, and only five to fifteen snakeheads.

"There's a lot of food in this system," says Odenkirk. "Right now we are not seeing the ecological and economic damage."

Of course, an invasive species can change an ecosystem over time, and any number of subtle changes could shift the balance toward snakehead dominance. It is too early to know, and it's understandable why people should feel uneasy about this aggressive predator.

What is interesting, though, is just how much of the spotlight the snakehead has commanded. It's a monster unleashed, unstoppable. Meanwhile, though, a far bigger danger to the Potomac, to all rivers, looms. Snakeheads may hide in the reeds, but the bigger threats to the river hide behind arguments that seem commonsensical. Certain politicians argue that laws like the Clean Water Act represent fiscal waste and bureaucratic overreach. Overregulation, they say, has destroyed the middle class, agriculture, industry, the economy. We've put fish before families.

Have we really forgotten those sludge-filled rivers? Was a time of fish kills and stinking water really our country at its greatest?

"We can't have sustainable, vibrant communities without clean water. We can't have the recreation and wildlife without clean water," says Hedrick Belin. "None of this is possible without clean water."

Belin, like many river advocates, fear calls to roll back Clean Water Act protections and other environmental regulations. They also fear more subtle attacks in the form of huge budget cuts. At the time of this writing, one budget proposal called for cutting Potomac River appropriations by as much as 90 percent.

"Without funding, you don't have the leadership, technical assistance, or enforcement of regulations," says Belin. "That would take away critical ingredients to the success we've seen on the Potomac."

The river restoration might be so successful that people take it for granted and don't realize that it would never have happened without regulations and funding.

"The recovery we've made is wonderful to see, but it's a fragile recovery," says Belin. "We can't afford to backslide. But we will without a local movement for clean water. Without the political will, without local advocates leading the fight, we will not be able to achieve lasting protection for this river."

After an afternoon of catching fish (and the requisite stop at an excellent Thai restaurant), Patrick and I stopped by his apartment to pick up Lia for more fishing. We headed back to the Capitol Mall with a list of nighttime feeders on our mind.

When most anglers celebrate the Potomac's recovery, they mention largemouth bass, striped bass, and shad. I had my sights set on a different denizen, but one no less emblematic of this river: the American eel.

Historically, eels made up a quarter of the total fish biomass in the Potomac, and they swam this river and its tributaries by the millions. Eels do the reverse of the migrations undertaken by fish like salmon and shad. They are born in the ocean; it was once even a mystery where exactly they spawned. It has now been determined that they congregate in the Sargasso Sea in the North Atlantic Ocean. The young eels migrate to freshwater, where they run up rivers and live out their adult lives. Years later, full grown and sexually mature, they return to the ocean to spawn.

Like other migratory fish, eel populations have been devastated by dams, by sediment, and by pollution of the kind that turned the Potomac into a cesspool. Even when the river recovered, they were commercially overharvested. Their US population is at 1 percent of historic levels, but a couple of million still run up the Potomac.

I remembered hearing my grandfather telling stories of catching eels with his dad along the Susquehanna River in Central Pennsylvania, near where I grew up. I could not imagine this slithering critter swimming my local waters, and by the time I began fishing, they were largely gone. There were just too many dams for them to navigate. I had harbored a desire to catch an eel ever since.

We arrived at the Capitol Mall at dusk, the tourist hordes beginning to dissipate. We set up a line of rods, each baited with nightcrawlers and rigged with slip sinkers. Lia's rod twitched first, and she reeled in a white perch, another native species found in the lower stretch of the Potomac, where the river is still influenced by tides. A few minutes later, I caught a white perch of my own.

My next strike bent my rod more sharply, and after a spirited fight, I landed a striped bass. "Not what we're after," Patrick said with a grin. A striped bass is a prized catch anywhere and forty years ago would have been a near impossibility in this stretch of river. Now they, too, have rebounded nicely.

I briefly looked at the fish, the Washington Monument literally providing the backdrop. I thought Washington, who for a time operated a commercial shad fishery, would have been proud that citizens still fight to keep these fish in the river.

I cast my line back out, a siren wailing in the distance. I have wilderness-advocate friends who dismiss urban fishing as a poor substitute for vast public lands, but the fact is that more people now live in cities than at any point in history. Wild experiences need to happen wherever you are, not just in pristine, remote places. We need advocates for clean water, everywhere, and that advocacy is going to come from love, not fear. And love comes from connection. Like setting up a fishing rod along a big-city river, waiting for an eel to bite.

My rod soon twitched again. I pulled up and set the hook, and this time my rod didn't so much as buck but *twist*. It felt like the fish was pulling straight back. Writhing. Patrick knew right away. "Don't lose this one," he said. "Don't."

I pushed away rising anxiety, as the writhing intensified and I wondered if it would twist my knots right off the line. And then it came in sight: an eel about 14 inches long. I hoisted it ashore. It looked nothing like the conventional notion of a "fish." It was tempting to compare it to a snake, and yet it really didn't resemble anything reptilian, either. A brief touch revealed it was as slimy as it looked. I stared at its beady eyes, its needle-sharp teeth.

I have encountered few fish, or any creatures, so utterly alien, so captivating. It continued wriggling and twisting, the Washington Monument still blinking in the background. I could only hope that we come to consider our environmental laws with the same pride we regard the achievements of our Founding Fathers. Encounters with eels and striped bass can remind us of what we almost lost forever, and what we certainly will lose again if we're not vigilant.

I released the eel into the Potomac, into its fragile, hopeful, uncertain future. It quickly disappeared into the darkness, as if a ghost. I lifted my rod, and cast again into the night.

Chapter Fourteen

Waiting for Sturgeon

A large truck passed just 3 feet behind me, shaking the bridge as it passed. As I rested against the guard rail, I contemplated how I could cast my rod without snagging these vehicles, or the various beams and cables that made up the bridge.

Sensing my confusion, Adam Goldberg walked over with my rod. "Do you know the underhand pier cast?" he asked.

I did not. He demonstrated with his long spinning rod, lowering it straight down off the bridge toward the water. "You wind back a bit, lean back, let go and yell WHOOOOOOP!" he exclaimed.

"The WHOOP is important," he emphasized. "It gives you an extra few feet."

Down the bridge, another voice. "Is that you, Goldberg?"

A group of high school students walked our way, to verify the source of the whoop. "Isn't it a school night?" Goldberg asked. "Shouldn't you be doing homework or something?"

The kids laughed at this ridiculous question. They wanted to catch a lake sturgeon. So did I.

I did my best to imitate Goldberg's cast, and my line sailed out and landed into the St. Croix River, on the Minnesota–Wisconsin border. Even without the whoop, it achieved plenty of distance.

I leaned my rod against the bridge piling. The anglers around me told jokes and fishing stories.

We waited. Sturgeon fishing, I would learn very quickly, was all about waiting. At times over the next couple of years, as I continued my pursuit of wild sturgeon, the waiting would drive me crazy. I'd have to remind myself that there were indeed still sturgeon out there, in the St. Croix River, and in waters closer to home. The possibility of catching one of these ancient fish kept me going.

Sturgeon are another fish that swam when dinosaurs roamed. Some species, including the lake sturgeon, can reach sizes larger than I am. They have an elongated snout and a low-slung mouth for bottom feeding. They have barbels—essentially, long whiskers—that are their taste buds. They use these to detect food on the bottom. Their skeletons consist of cartilage, but they're covered in bony plates that can feel like armor. North America has nine species, including the white sturgeon found in the Snake River near my home. I had been intimidated by the tactics required to catch a fish that can reach 12 feet long, and had delayed trying. As I contemplated sturgeon, I received an invite from Alex Orr, the Vader-tattooed life lister who had caught a chiselmouth with me, to join him in Minnesota for a fall fishing trip.

I met him on a sunny October day at an old farmhouse outside of St. Paul, where he lives with his mom, brothers, and girlfriend. One of his brothers was leaving to go bowhunting as I arrived. Fishing rods and traps rested against the garage. Alex came out of the house, waving all around. "Some people want to move away from their family as soon as possible," he said. "I love living here. We all love the outdoors. We look out for each other."

I soon met his girlfriend, Maggie, a hard-core roughfisher Alex met through an online fishing forum, and brother Quinn, a rapper who produces albums under the name $mQKey. We grabbed rods and piled into the car. My initial assessment of Alex as an especially generous person held true, as he refused to let me pay for so much as worms. He lent me his finest fishing gear, bought me great Mexican food, and showed me his primo spots.

And he talked fishing. I've met a lot of dedicated anglers while traveling for this book, but I'm not sure any love the sport as much as Alex. When I mentioned this to him, he laughed. "I spent some time in prison when I was younger," he said. "I was a pretty bad dude. Now, life revolves around fishing."

We drove into Wisconsin to a stream that Alex knew contained a large population of greater redhorse, a beefy, hard-fighting sucker species often coveted by the life listing community. I saw suckers finning right below a little country bridge. I dropped my line in the water and immediately felt the tug of the fish. After several powerful runs, I reeled in my first greater redhorse. Within a few minutes, Alex and Quinn had both caught large redhorses themselves. As cool as these fish were, though, this was really just a warm-up for the main event. A night-time quest for lake sturgeon.

As darkness settled, we pulled into a parking lot along the St. Croix River, quiet but for the sound of vehicles rumbling over the bridge. A bearded man with an impish grin strode across the lot waving his hand, and Alex smiled. This was when I first met Adam Goldberg, a bit of a legend in the roughfishing and life listing community. That's in part because he has an uncanny ability to find fish. But more so, he has a boundless optimism about everything he does and everyone he meets. A self-described "redneck Hebrew," his truck was festooned with stickers advertising his love of guns, hunting, and fishing, including a large decal of a gar.

"The river has been slow lately," Alex said, and warned me against getting my hopes up.

"Don't worry, we'll get one," Goldberg said. "If we have to stay out all night, we'll get one."

We spent the first couple of hours on the bridge, period-ically checking our lines, Goldberg whooping when he recast. We jammed several nightcrawlers onto large hooks but nothing so much as tapped our baits. The other anglers lining the bridge didn't have any better luck. They all stuck it out, hoping for an encounter with one of the 6-foot monsters that fed along the river's bottom.

An autumn chill descended on the river, and we huddled into our coats. Around 11:00 p.m., Alex apologized but said he had to get some sleep. He and his crew departed, as did the high school students. Goldberg and I remained. After more waiting, Goldberg suggested we move to a little cove where he'd had some luck recently.

We walked over there, cast our baits, and waited some more. We talked about fishing and hunting, about road trips and rivers. The time passed quickly and I started to wonder if Goldberg was serious about staying out all night.

My line twitched. Despite their large size, sturgeon bite softly. I lifted my line and felt a light struggle. I reeled in and found a foot-long, plump mudpuppy—a large, brown-patterned sala-mander—on my line. I was more than happy with this bizarre catch, and figured it was enough for the night.

"You get tired of catching them here," said Goldberg. "But I admit, they're cool looking. Let's give it a bit more time."

More waiting. And then another tap. I lifted my rod and again felt a light struggle. I suspected another mudpuppy. But then whatever it was made a spirited run. It was not an amphibian.

As it got closer, Goldberg exclaimed, "Sturgeon!"

As I reeled up, I saw it was an 18-inch fish. A young one, but nonetheless my first sturgeon. "Be careful handling it," Goldberg said. "The little ones have sharp plates."

I lifted it gingerly, marveling at the prehistoric creature in my hands. The combination of bony plates, long snout, and whiskers gave the fish an otherworldly appearance. I gently released it back into the water.

It was 1:00 a.m. Goldberg apologized that we had not caught a larger fish, but I was more than satisfied with this encounter. In fact, just to be out fishing for sturgeon is the sign of a major con-servation achievement.

Twenty-seven species of sturgeon were once common in rivers across North America, Europe, and Asia. In modern times, they have not fared well. In fact, the International Union for the Conservation of Nature (IUCN), the agency that keeps track of endangered species, considers sturgeon the most imperiled group of animals on earth. More than 85 percent of sturgeon species are threatened or endangered, including every species that lives in Europe and Asia.

Sturgeon face threats familiar to freshwater species, including dams and pollution. In Eurasia, they also face the added threat of poaching for caviar. As with ivory, the rarity of caviar commands high prices, fueling organized crime. Some Eurasian sturgeon species are among the most endangered fish in the world.

In North America, the lake sturgeon seemed destined for a similar fate. Once common in the Upper Mississippi watershed, the Minnesota DNR compares them to bison in their historical importance to local Indian tribes. Like the bison, this abundance was wiped out as European colonists headed west. In the mid-1800s, a caviar industry developed for lake sturgeon, and writer Michael Kallok notes in the *Minnesota Conservation Volunteer* that nearly 1 million pounds of sturgeon was harvested in just one year in Lake of the Woods in northern Minnesota. He writes, "In addition to the roe, fish processors began selling sturgeon meat, skin for leather, and isinglass—a gelatinous substance in its swim bladder—for clarifying wine and beer."

Fish populations declined rapidly, to the point that commercial harvest was no longer profitable. Despite the lack of fishing pressure, populations didn't rebound. Sturgeon mature very slowly, and don't spawn every year. The imperiled sturgeon was then hit with dams and declining water quality due to sewage and industrial development. By the early 1900s, lake sturgeon had disappeared from numerous waters in Minnesota.

This story has a happy ending. Like the Potomac River, waters in Minnesota like the St. Croix benefited heavily from the Clean

Water Act. Conservationists worked with agencies to remove dams that were no longer necessary. And an effort began to restock waters with lake sturgeon. They survived and prospered, so much so that some rivers—including the section of the St. Croix where I caught my sturgeon—allow a limited, carefully regulated harvest of fish.

A similarly hopeful story played out in neighboring Wisconsin's Lake Winnebago. In 1915, the state's newly created Conservation Commission outlawed all sturgeon harvest, considered an extraordinary step at the time. In 1930, commercial fishermen removing carp from Lake Winnebago reported incidentally netting a lot of lake sturgeon. Sportsmen believed that they could responsibly resume the local tradition of spearing sturgeon through the ice. They lobbied the legislature, which enacted a limited spearing season.

That spearing season continues to this day, a tradition recounted in the book by Kathleen Schmitt Kline and sturgeon researchers Ronald Bruch and Frederick Binkowski, *People of the Sturgeon.* Unlike many wildlife laws that treat people as adversaries, the sturgeon spearing program has relied on a partnership between state resource managers and the local community. While most sturgeon teeter on the brink, Lake Winnebago's sturgeon population thrives.

After catching my first sturgeon with Goldberg, my thoughts turned to sturgeon closer to home. The Snake River that flows through Idaho was legendary for its salmon and steelhead runs, but it also was home to a thriving white sturgeon population. The dams built on the Snake and the Columbia rivers are among the most reviled among environmentalists, and again that attention focuses largely on salmon and steelhead. But sturgeon have suffered, too.

Unlike salmon, sturgeon have a difficult time negotiating fish ladders. Many are simply too large. White sturgeon still spawn in the Pacific Northwest. States like Oregon and Washington even allow harvest. Idaho has just two stretches of the Snake River where the sturgeon spawn.

But they do not reproduce in the sturgeon water closest to my home, the middle stretch of the Snake River. Sturgeon require specific water quality and flow to spawn. The Middle Snake contains several dams, restricting sturgeon movement. Even if the sturgeon do spawn successfully, the young sturgeon immediately run into problems. That's because after they hatch, young sturgeon drift downriver. In the Middle Snake, the distance between dams is such that they soon find themselves in reservoirs. For sturgeon fry, the churning, turbid waters of the flowing Snake protect them from predators. In the calm waters of the reservoir, native and non-native fish munch them like candy. They have no chance.

Idaho Power, the utility that operates the dams, works with the Idaho Department of Fish and Game on sturgeon conservation. The highest priority is protecting the two spawning populations. But there is also the recognition that even if sturgeon can't successfully spawn on the Middle Snake, they can still survive quite well. Some wild sturgeon, after all, have lived in these river stretches for decades. In the mid-1990s, Idaho Power and the state agency decided to supplement these fish, stocking sturgeon in the Middle Snake and providing an opportunity for anglers.

Wild sturgeon are captured during the spawning season and delivered to the College of Southern Idaho's aquaculture facility, where they are spawned out and reared until they reach a foot in length. Then they're released in the Middle Snake River.

In other locations, fish stocking is done either on a "put-and-take" basis—where anglers are expected to catch and keep the fish—or with the idea of establishing a breeding population of fish. The Middle Snake sturgeon program is neither. The fish will not breed, and the fishing is strictly catch and release. Through the decades of a sturgeon's life, it will likely be caught many times.

"It's been a very, very popular fishery," says Phil Bates, Idaho Power fisheries biologist. "Providing a recreational fishery is an important component of the Middle Snake's sturgeon program."

Hoping to avoid the crowds that such popularity brings, I chose a weekday for my first foray to the river below C. J. Strike Dam, one of the stretches stocked with white sturgeon. My thoughts of sturgeon solitude were quickly dashed. RVs lined the access, and senior citizens sat by large, big-game fishing rods stuck into PVC tubes that had been driven into the ground. Some chatted at nearby picnic tables, barely watching their rods. Others sat in lawn chairs, sipping Cokes or light beer as they watched their rod tips. It resembled a retirement community built around sturgeon fishing. They all looked like people who had plenty of time to wait.

I found an open spot and set up my own rod. I looked into the water: big, churning, intimidating. I saw an eddy where the water looked deeper, and cast there. Then I, too, joined the waiting.

I lacked the friends, spouses, and grandkids of the other anglers. I also didn't have a nearby RV for periodic snack breaks or card games. After a few hours, boredom settled in. I had not had anything that I could even pretend was a nibble.

The other sturgeon anglers didn't have any better luck. I watched them, hoping I could glean some strategy from what they were doing. I was struck by the similarity of everyone's tackle and rigs. This was not by accident.

Even catch-and-release angling can kill sturgeon if the fish aren't treated properly, which could lead to a complete prohibition on fishing. Regulations required barbless hooks, attached to a line that also had a sliding sinker on a separate, lighter line. This way, if the line snagged, the weight would break. If a hook was left dangling to a heavy weight in the water, a sturgeon could eat it and not be able to free itself, dying on the bottom of the river.

Anglers also are prohibited from removing fish from the water for any reason, including photos. This rule, especially in the age of social media, can be difficult for anglers to follow.

"Fortunately, sturgeon anglers are great at self-policing," says Joe Kozfkay, Southwest Region fish manager for the Idaho Department of Fish and Game. "If they see someone trying to lift up a sturgeon or drag it ashore, they'll let the person know."

Since the sturgeon's skeletal structure consists of cartilage, large fish can be injured if they're hoisted. "Sturgeon don't have a robust, bony skeleton," says Ken Lepla, another Idaho Power fisheries biologist who works on sturgeon issues. "For the large sturgeon, it can really stress them being lifted. In any case, I think the best photos are those of an angler in the water beside a large fish."

Handled carefully, sturgeon survive the release. Joe Kozfkay says that angler surveys suggest that the average sturgeon in the Middle Snake is hooked eight times and landed four during any given year.

But not by me. I sat and waited. Checked my bait, recast, and waited. And watched other anglers waiting. A few bass and panfish anglers arrived and had better luck, tempting me to break out my ultralight rod. This temptation deepened when a guy started casting a light rod close to me, catching yellow perch and crappies on nearly every cast. I remained steadfast in my hopes of a sturgeon.

After seven hours, I decided to end the outing. As I packed up my gear, the perch fisher next to me let out a yodel. His rod was bent so far I was sure it would shatter. He reeled furiously. "Honey, I got a sturgeon!" he yelled.

It was about 2 feet, a small one but nonetheless a sturgeon. He followed the rules, releasing it in the water. It was the first white sturgeon I had seen landed all day.

I made another cast, now hopeful. But no fish showed. I left in the dark, the sound of the waters churning below the dam echoing across the canyon.

~

For many environmentalists, nothing is quite as enraging as a dam. Replacing a free-flowing river, a complex ecosystem, with a concrete monstrosity seems like one of the ultimate desecrations of nature. The loss of salmon runs, and sturgeon, top the list of dam casualties.

For anglers, feelings about dams are mixed. More than a few reservoirs exist largely to supply sport fishing. Trout anglers, who gush over flowing water, eschew these human-made lakes. But they flock to the waters rushing out of dams—tailwaters—including some of the most revered fly-fishing rivers in the world. The cold water released from dams create perfect conditions for aquatic insects and the trout that feed on them.

I've heard environmentalist friends say they wish dams didn't exist. It's an appealing sentiment, but it ignores just how prevalent dams are. In the United States, there are an estimated eighty-four thousand dams. That's right: eighty-four thousand. Many provide hydropower and irrigation. We will not live in a world without dams.

Around the world, many other countries are following our pattern of hydropower development. Even on river systems many of us consider the most remote places on Earth, extensive dams are planned. There will be dams in the Congo Basin and dams on the Amazon.

Hopefully, these countries can learn from our mistakes. Dams do not have to completely destroy migratory fisheries. They can be constructed in places that minimize impact. They can incorporate state-of-the-art fish passage devices.

The science is available. And it can be applied to existing dams as well as new ones. In the United States, there have been promising efforts to evaluate dams and to see how they can be improved for migratory fish. Conservationists have found that among those eighty-four thousand dams are many that are no longer necessary. Some provided service to mills in the 1700s but have not been utilized in a century. Others have fallen into disrepair, providing no commercial purpose but nonetheless stopping fish.

My day-job employer, The Nature Conservancy, has had some notable successes in dam removal, including the recent restoration of the Pawcatuck River in southern Rhode Island. Four dams had blocked this river for fish migration since the 1760s. The Conservancy and partners removed three of the dams and built a fish passage on a fourth. The local community embraced the project, and fish have begun returning.

In many places, dam removal is not politically feasible or even desirable, but some dams could be made more amenable for fish movement. In Florida, my colleague Steve Herrington observed that Alabama shad, a migratory fish, could pass through shipping locks on the Apalachicola River. The problem was, shad cue in on the sound of running water, which they don't hear in the locks.

He devised a system that used a generator to pump a stream of water through PVC pipe and into the shipping lock. The sound of splashing water drew the shad into the lock and enabled them to access the upper parts of the river. The number of fish able to pass through the dam increased from 10,000 to 250,000, a conservation success achieved with low-cost products that could be purchased at the local Home Depot.

Dams are a part of our world. Increasingly, we will have the technology to improve existing dams and make new ones more fish-friendly. Still, in some areas, native fish will struggle. Efforts like sturgeon stocking in the Middle Snake will remain a part of the angling scene.

—⁓—

Many of the fish species that appear in this book presented challenges to me as an angler. For the most part, if I stuck with it, I eventually caught them. Patience pays off. Sometimes it was in the last hour, or even on the "last cast," but I caught the fish.

But not a white sturgeon. I kept at it, but I admit that after a while my enthusiasm flagged. Sturgeon fishing requires patience, perhaps more than I possess. Nonetheless, don't be surprised if you run into me with a large rod below C. J. Strike Dam.

I've found that it's good to have fish that remain just out of reach. Your own personal Moby Dick. A fish that frustrates you, makes you question your skill and devotion. A fish in the depths that is still out there, if only you put in enough time.

As I continued to fish for wild sturgeon, though, I learned of another place. This place reveals another truth of 21st-century fishing: that just about anything can be had, easily, for a price. And that includes white sturgeon.

CHAPTER FIFTEEN

Down on the Sturgeon Ranch

I stopped my car in front of a sign advertising "Redneck Gifts" as a couple of barking farm dogs circled the car. Within seconds, a screen door swung open and a stout, heavily bearded man in coveralls waved me out of the car.

"Jim Schwartz," he offered, holding out a calloused hand. "You here to do some fishing?"

"I am."

"Then you came to the wrong place," he said, a frown crossing his face.

He stared intently, sensing the confusion. A grin replaced the scowl.

"We don't offer fishing here, we offer catching!" he boomed.

"You'll catch fish here, all right," he continued. "Had a fellow this weekend catch eighty-nine, but he knows what he's doing. If you're really lucky, you'll catch Tony. He's a 7-footer. Catch him and you come next time for free."

I had entered the realm where the fish you catch have names. Schwartz grabbed a large container of wine-marinated herring— "They go crazy for this"—and motioned me to follow him on his ATV. We drove past chicken pens and farm implements to his 2-acre farm pond, a not unusual feature in this part of agricultural southwestern Idaho.

But the draw here wasn't the usual bass, bluegills, and bullheads. Schwartz's Pond, as it is known, is stocked with white sturgeon, the same fish that had outwitted me so many times on the nearby Snake River. For just $25, you could tangle with your own river monster. Actually: many river monsters. Unlike the wild and unruly Snake, here you never need guess where the sturgeon are.

Schwartz dug out the pond several years ago. He previously offered fee pond fishing for catfish and bluegill, but wanted a bigger draw. Something you could not catch just anywhere.

Water from irrigation canals fed a pond that looked like a bulldozer had just gouged a hole in the ground. Few trees lined its bank, and sections were roped off to get grass seed established. A couple of wooden benches and assorted plastic chairs sat along the edge.

Schwartz stopped his ATV and hopped out, grabbing a handful of fish pellets. He tossed them into the pond. "This will get 'em feeding," he said. "This is where they've been catching them, but don't be afraid to move around."

A fish splashed in the middle of the pond. "Do you know why sturgeon jump?" he asked. He didn't wait for me to answer. "They're giving you the fin."

In addition to offering sturgeon fishing, Jim Schwartz writes outdoor humor books and sells redneck-themed knickknacks. He usually stays by the pond to assist guests, but today, Schwartz told me, he'd just check in periodically due to some pressing farm chores. He gave me some pointers on setting the hook on sturgeon—"It takes most people a few bites before they get the hang of it"—then he wished me luck and zipped away.

I baited my large, barbless hook with the wine-soaked herring and cast my catfish rod into the pond. A minute later, my rod tip started tap-tap-tapping. I lifted up and . . . nothing.

I reeled in and found my bait gone. I cast again and even more quickly had a bite. And even more quickly lost my bait. I pulled out more stinky herring and cast again. This time, my tip jerked sharply. I lifted the rod and had a fish on. As I reeled it in, it looked nothing like a sturgeon. It was a big rainbow trout, although not much of a match for the stout spinning rod I carried.

I slipped the hook out of the fish's lip, released it, and quickly got my line back in the water. Within a few minutes, my rod tip made a subtle bounce. I lifted up and felt another fish. I could tell immediately that it wasn't large, but it wasn't a trout. It made a short, deep run, but I quickly reeled it in.

My first white sturgeon. A small one, maybe 20 inches, but a sturgeon. Schwartz forbids fish being lifted from the water, and I wanted to quickly release it, but I glanced over the fish before me. It looked utterly alien, with a long snout festooned with whiskers and a back that looked as if it was covered in armor. Prehistoric.

I cast again and waited ten minutes, my longest period without a bite. This time, my rod made sharper jerks, and as I set the hook, I knew I had a larger fish. It made a bullish run, peeling off line. Tip up, pressure on, but the fish kept going.

After a few minutes, the runs became shorter, and by reeling toward the fish, then lifting the rod, and repeating, I tired it. This one was nearly 4 feet, one of the larger fish I've caught in Idaho. I slipped out the barbless hook and the sturgeon swam back into the pond's depths.

I continued to reel in fish. I heard the sound of the ATV and Schwartz pulled up. "Arms tired yet?" he asked.

"Caught five so far," I said.

"That's all? You need to move around," he replied. He stayed to watch me cast, as if assessing my now-suspect fishing skills.

I had seen the social media posts before my visit, the ones describing this as "fishing heaven." A place where an angler, any skill level, could tangle with huge, rare fish all day long. A place where five sturgeon before lunch qualifies as a failure. Is this the utopian vision of our fishing future? Or is it one step closer to the apocalypse?

I did not come to Schwartz's Pond to tick "white sturgeon" off my life list. If I couldn't catch a wild one, it wouldn't count.

I visited because I realized that here was a very real vision for fishing's future in the United States. In fact, it's already more a part of the present picture than many anglers are comfortable admitting.

Often called pay lakes or fee ponds, this form of fishing is usually associated with trout, and kids. There are small ponds in many parts of the country, often near popular tourist attractions, where you check in with an attendant, drop a line and catch fish. A lot of fish.

Many of these are little more than concrete hatchery runs, with similar aesthetics and ambience. Kids, of course, don't care. As anyone who has taken a toddler fishing knows, there's a somewhat short attention span between fish. The pay lake solves this by eliminating wait time.

The fun comes at a price. At most of these ponds, you have to keep what you catch, and you pay by the pound. My brother-in-law took my nephews, Jacob and Jack, to one of these facilities and they racked up more than $50 worth of trout in fifteen minutes. The kids wanted to keep on catching. None of this is dissimilar to the hatchery system of "put-and-take" fishing previously discussed.

Now put that same pond in the shadow of the Rockies, add some nice landscaping, and situate it next to a spacious lodge decked out in sporting memorabilia: presto, the hatchery pond becomes a bastion of sport. And maybe the clientele tends toward scotch and cigars more than candy bars and Cokes, and the guides wear breathable Simms jackets rather than ratty T-shirts, but let's face it: it's still a pay pond.

These ponds are less obvious but they're often situated near "destination" trout rivers. If the conditions are tough—or the client can't cast—the guest can still take home plenty of trophy photos by fishing the lodge's "private waters." The angler will have a stellar day fishing "sow bug" patterns that bear a striking resemblance to fish pellets—if anyone cared to look closely. Which no one ever does.

Around the South, pay lakes have popped up offering anglers the chance to catch catfish. While some of these fish, like the trout, are farmed, it's difficult to grow a catfish to trophy size in the short time period required to replace fish. So many pay pond owners have turned to commercial fishers who still ply large, wild rivers. These operations catch plenty of large channel, blue, and flathead catfish—some of them trophy size— and these are then stocked in the lakes for eager anglers looking to battle a monster.

Of course, many anglers seek large wild catfish recreationally in rivers and lakes. They see pay ponds as depleting their trophy fish, and a public resource, for no reason other than to supply less-skilled anglers a steady supply of fillets.

In England and across much of continental Europe, pay lakes are an accepted part of the fishing scene. Many of the prime fishing waters, especially for trout, have long been reserved for the royal and wealthy. Public fishing is far more limited than in the United States. The pay lakes offer an alternative, and have developed their own angling culture.

In Europe, *the* game fish is carp. This is strictly catch-and-release fishing, and carp are wily, so they become extraordinarily wary about being hooked. This necessitates tactics like hair rigs, where the bait is threaded to a hair, then tied to a hook so that the fish sucks in the bait without actually feeling extra weight or metal.

Anglers use specially formulated dough baits, sometimes concocting "pack baits" that slowly dissolve in the water by a hooked piece of corn. This gets the fish feeding with confidence right around the bait. There are alarms that alert the angler to the lightest nibble, and soft, moistened mats that allow fish to be photographed before release.

In certain ponds, fish grow obese and are given names—sometimes becoming legends in the process. Unlike most pay pond fishing in the United States, the fishing requires supreme angling skills and patience.

England's pay lake scene arose due to a lack of fishing opportunities. It's a model that's spread around the world, even creating angling destinations. As is the case in Thailand.

With its warm climate and history of aquaculture, Thailand has become the pay pond equivalent of an African safari. Many of the ponds host a variety of carp and catfish species, most notably the critically endangered Mekong giant catfish. Here, anglers can tangle with a species nearly extinct in the wild.

Other venues offer the chance to catch some of the world's most exotic fish species. Anglers at pay ponds might hook arapaima, the "river monster" of the Amazon, or alligator gar from the American South, or barramundi from Australia, or snakeheads from local Thai waters.

Traveling anglers book special trips to catch as many species as possible. The parallels to canned hunts are difficult to avoid.

I have friends who attribute this whole scene to laziness, or decadence, or both. The American sportsman, they believe, spouts off about being close to nature and living a rugged, outdoor lifestyle but in reality just wants to kill stuff. Look at the "hunting preserves" where "sportsmen" blast genetically modified deer in small pens. Look at stocked trout. Look at pay ponds.

But could it be something more? Once, the world abounded in fish and game. Every stream was blue ribbon, every river chock full of migrating fish. Trout weren't selective. Big fish were the norm. Now, finding the best waters often requires long travel, or specialized gear, or both.

When an operator offers all the big fish you can catch for $25, isn't it just replicating the good old days? Isn't it providing more opportunity to experience the fun of catching fish?

—◆—

Because, I had to admit as my drag squealed, battling big fish *is* fun. By afternoon, the day had warmed considerably, and the sturgeon bite had picked up. Each cast yielded bites, and I found myself reeling in fish large and small.

This pond definitely was of the no-frills variety, but according to Schwartz, it had begun drawing anglers from England, Australia, Japan, and other countries. "They love the country setting, too," he told me during one of his check-ins.

I looked around at this piece of Canyon County, Idaho, and wondered whether this was any more "real country" than the pond offered "real fishing." In one direction, a large, confined dairy, home to thousands of Holsteins, sprawled across a field. On my drive in, I saw a surprising number of these factory farms dotting the landscape. I could hear the sound of roosters crowing. Shots periodically rang out, either someone shooting targets or marmots. But it was hard to ignore the subdivisions popping up and snaking toward Schwartz's Pond.

While Idaho contains 60 percent public land, this part of the state had been predominantly farmland. Boise, the fastest growing city in the country, sat just to the east, and each year more prime agricultural ground gave way to houses. Many people moved here for "country living," despite living in developments that displaced real country. Residents appeared to keep the rural atmosphere alive through purchasing large trucks, ATVs, boats, and lots of outdoor gear. They just needed a place to use it.

One of these nearby residents soon pulled up in a jacked-up, muddied pickup. A guy in his early twenties, wearing a camo sweatshirt and factory-scuffed hat, confidently hopped out and surveyed the pond with a wry smile. Soon his trim girlfriend, wearing a pink shirt with the Browning logo and a similarly scuffed hat, stood beside him.

"Aw baby, this is what I've been waiting to show you," he said, gesturing to the pond around him. "This is what I live for."

His truck still ran, pumping out modern country. And it soon became apparent that this guy saw himself as the living embodiment of that music, a curious mix of down-home reverence mixed unironically with a celebration of hell-raising. And plenty of redneck clichés.

He pulled a pre-rigged rod out of the back. He nodded seriously at me across the narrow pond as I fought a fish. The look suggested I might have stolen something from him, perhaps hooked the last sturgeon that Jim Schwartz owned.

He quickly cast and propped up his rod in one of Schwartz's PVC rod holders, then turned his attention to his girlfriend. "Remember what I taught you, baby," he said, his voice carrying across the water.

She wound back the rod like it was a baseball bat and launched the bait right at her feet. "No, like this," he said, and cast the rod for her. He then began barking orders like a drill sergeant, with predictable results. She missed fish. He groaned.

He turned his attention to his own rod, now doubled with a fish. "That's what I'm talking about," he said with been-here-before cool.

He landed and released the small sturgeon, and then his girlfriend once again lifted up the rod. "I think I have something," she said calmly.

No calm now for the boyfriend. "Tip up, reel, no not now, reel now. Tip up, baby. Tip up!" He continued hollering instructions, loud enough to bring Schwartz back to the pond. He joined in with encouraging shouts. "You got this! Keep reeling, it's tiring! Tip up!"

Soon the sturgeon was by her side. As with the regulations for wild sturgeon, Schwartz doesn't allow the fish to be lifted from the water, so the young woman knelt beside it in the water for the obligatory photo.

"First sturgeon?" Schwartz asked.

"First fish ever," she replied.

"Now that's what I like to hear! How many people can say their first fish was a white sturgeon? You're starting at the top."

The boyfriend, now relaxed, gave his girlfriend a hug and leaned back to take it all in. Soon we were all hooking and landing fish. Schwartz stuck around.

By now, the boyfriend had entered the fishing philosophy stage. "It's a wonder no one made fishing a religion," he said. "It feels pretty religious to me."

"Ever heard of Jesus?" Schwartz asked. "Know how he fed all those hungry people? Fish. Sounds like a religion about fishing to me."

"Pretty deep. Never thought about that."

Then his rod doubled over and it was clear he had a big one on. "I have Tony! It's Tony!" he exclaimed.

"Not quite," Schwartz responded laconically. "But still a good fish."

What followed was fifteen minutes of whooping and hooting seemingly more suited to a football game. I had a fish of my own on, but it slipped the barbless hook. I was out of bait, so I just watched the young man wear down the fish, bring it in, and whoop some more.

As the fish finally swam away, he pumped his fist to his chest. "This is my Viagra, man," he yelled. "This is what it's all about!"

The girlfriend looked back at her line, clearly uncomfortable with this turn in the fishing. But as I walked by them to depart the ranch, both wore big, happy smiles. "Saw you catch some, too," the boyfriend said. "Special place, isn't it? I wanted my girl-friend to see it for herself. I think she gets it now. This is what it's all about."

He gestured to the pond in front of him, to the sturgeon now regularly roiling the surface. Here he was, experiencing the great outdoor life.

I didn't know how to respond. Yes, I admit again, hooking and fighting a big fish is fun, on a visceral level. But, ultimately, visiting the pond turned fishing into a trivial pursuit, divorced from any meaningful connection to the natural world. Is this what it's all about?

I walked away from my whooping fellow anglers, and I wondered: If this was the only fishing left, would I still do it?

And I couldn't find an honest answer, other than this: It doesn't have to come to that. Even in our growing, human-filled world, it doesn't have to come to that.

Chapter Sixteen

Abundance

Never did rotting fish smell so good. The scent lingered everywhere, overpowering even the fragrant pine trees lining the river. As I ran along the sandbar, fly rod arched high over my head, I stepped on fish carcass after fish carcass, interspersed with imposing bear tracks. In the riffles, the red forms of salmon pushed up the river. On my line, a large fish—likely a Dolly Varden char—rushed downstream, trying to shake its connection to me.

I attempted to concentrate on the fish, to gain line and get it in without falling into the river. And yet I found myself trying to take it all in, all this abundance. Because it really doesn't get much better, not if you have a passion for fish and fishing.

There's still a lot of great fishing in North America, but nothing can match the epic nature of Alaska's salmon runs—still here, still feeding an entire ecosystem. That's not to say that Alaska is without challenges, or that it has somehow escaped the influence of modern humanity. Even here, some rivers rely on hatchery salmon. Management can be especially complicated, balancing the differing priorities of commercial, Tribal, and recreational fishers. Most of all, an undeveloped land rich in resources cannot escape the attention of a ravenous and growing global society.

Still, you can almost forget those problems once you're on the river.

My dad turned seventy-five in the spring, and he asked me to pick a special outdoor trip for us to share. He wanted us to have fun and hopefully to have some success, as we experienced some recent hunting trips notable for their lack of game. My dad had not been fishing in fifteen years or so, and even before that, his angling had been irregular and casual. I couldn't think of a better place for a trip than Alaska. We reserved a spot at the Great Alaska Adventure Lodge, on the Kenai River.

You go to the Kenai, and most rivers in Alaska, for the salmon. Five species—chinook, silver, sockeye, chum, and pink—still run up rivers in astonishing numbers. They're born in these rivers, and after they've grown a bit, they head to the sea. Their return voyage is also their last; they'll reach their birth place, spawn, and die. Fresh from the sea, their flesh is still firm. While they have ceased feeding, they'll strike lures, either out of instinct or rage.

We spent our first days at the lodge chasing the silver salmon migrating up the river. One morning, my dad and I joined a Florida angler for some salmon trolling, the fishing equivalent of a meat hunt. Large lures wiggled behind the boat, and periodically the rods doubled over. The nearest angler began reeling. Within two hours, the three of us had landed our limits of three fish apiece.

With declining fish populations, angling pressure, and health concerns like mercury contamination, it can be easy to forget that fishing is a food-gathering activity. Catch and release is not really a sign of enlightenment; it's just the reality of an overcrowded and industrialized world. Most of the fish I caught during the course of this book went back into the water, but I'm still enjoying those salmon fillets.

We fell into the pleasant routine of catching fish during the day, while enjoying lodge life in the evenings. There were some groups of friends, but most of the clientele consisted of fathers and sons, here for the same reasons we were. It's hard to be in a bad mood when you're catching fish on a beautiful river. Even the expected rain never showed.

After catching plenty of salmon for the freezer, my attention turned from salmon to things that eat salmon. The salmon here nourish, well, just about everything. Even the trees here are fertilized by salmon. Anyone who has watched PBS nature documentaries know bears gorge on the fish, sometimes catching leaping fish as they surge up waterfalls. The big brown bears are certainly the most dramatic predators here (or, really, anywhere), but they're not the only participants in this moveable feast. The Kenai is a full-on salmon-binging orgy.

We saw this every day, everywhere we looked. Eagles ripped at carcasses in trees; while gulls fought over gobs of flesh. As we drove south out of Anchorage, pods of beluga whales breached as they hunted salmon in Cook Inlet. On the river, our fishing would be periodically interrupted with a seal popping out its head with a mouthful of sushi. Mergansers and loons dove for juvenile fish. Everything was bulking up on the fish carcasses floating down the river and rotting on banks and sandbars. Death and renewal, everywhere.

Beneath the water's surface, more feasting occurred—rainbow trout and Dolly Varden char set up shop downstream of spawning salmon, gulping both eggs and pieces of flesh. They grew to enormous sizes. Dolly Vardens in particular caught my fancy; they're decorated with a beautiful palette of colors like brook trout (also a char species), with deep-red bellies when they're spawning. They fight like bulldogs, tenacious and sulking. And they're ravenous.

A study by Nathan Furey at the University of British Columbia on the closely related bull trout (another char species) in a Canadian river with large salmon runs found that these predators could eat 5–12 percent of their body weight in a given day. Smaller bull trout held in lab tanks could eat 10–30 percent of their body weights in a day. That is like a 180-pound person eating 18–60 pounds. The researchers examined bull trout stomachs containing as many as sixty young salmon.

On the Kenai in September, the Dolly Vardens also binge, and floating a plastic bead that looks like an egg elicits savage strikes. I asked the lodge to arrange a day of fly fishing for char and rainbow trout. The one issue: my seventy-five-year-old dad had never cast a fly rod. He said he'd be happy just to ride in the drift boat and watch.

We met Taylor, our guide for the day, early the next morning over a hearty lodge breakfast of sausage, potatoes, and eggs. My dad said he would just be along for the ride. "I'll have you fly fishing in fifteen minutes," Taylor said. "Don't worry. You'll have a blast."

Most mornings, we'd just walk down the hill and hop in a boat, but today we headed far upriver, where only nonmotorized craft was allowed. We drove for forty-five minutes, my dad snoring most of the way. When we arrived, another drift boat was launching, and we could hear a yell of "Bear!" and saw the guide pointing to brush, only about 50 yards downstream of where we stood. "We'd better get in the boat," Taylor said.

He oared the boat downstream through riffles. Our lines were rigged plastic "eggs" pegged a half inch above the hook so a fish would be unlikely to swallow it before being hooked (making a safe release easier).

I dropped my fly line over the side and quickly caught a couple of small Dolly Vardens. Then Taylor pulled alongside a sandbar. "Here's the main event," he said. Carcasses lined the bank. Red sockeye salmon in various states of disrepair finned in a shallow side channel. They were literally rotting alive, some with globs of flesh hanging at their sides. The Swimming Dead.

A closer look at the salmon revealed that many, both alive and dead, sported hefty bite marks. One could imagine a bear ambling along, lazily taking a chomp out of each fish. Taylor set my dad up in some calmer water at the head of the sandbar. I headed down to a riffle, where he suggested I cast out to the edge of the churning water.

I flipped out my line and my indicator immediately bobbed under. In the rapids, the fish rushed downstream, forcing me to run with it, rod held high in the air for leverage. Periodically, it would stop and I could feel it shaking its head, the characteristic run of a nice char. As I reeled it in, I could see the beautiful spotted fish, the burnt red of its belly. Taylor netted it and snapped a quick photo, all without removing it from the water. He flipped the net and the fish swam free.

It wasn't a fish on every cast, but every few drifts the indicator would disappear and I'd have a nice fish on. Once my reel screamed as a fish started leaping downstream, a beautiful rainbow. At 20 inches, it was not as big as fish in some of Alaska's more remote rivers, but a bragging fish on most of the Idaho waters I usually frequent.

As if to spice things up further, on my next cast, my line screamed off even faster. I ran downriver until a steep drop-off halted my progress. I could hear Tyler urging me to fight it more aggressively. I could soon see why: it was a large sockeye salmon, bright red and humped. Such a fish would not be edible, and it ate its last meal long ago. Even during the height of the sockeye run, many anglers catch their fish by "flossing," running a fly by the fish's mouth, and then setting the hook. While snagging in the body is illegal, a fish can be kept if it's hooked in the mouth—even though this method amounts to mouth snagging. But sometimes the sockeyes strike an egg or lure out of aggression, and as I got this sockeye to the bank, I could see it was fairly hooked inside the mouth.

I had been so engrossed in the fishing that I hadn't even checked on my dad. I looked up and saw him whipping out nice casts on the seven-weight fly rod. He looked relaxed and experienced. I saw his indicator dip and his fly rod lift: he had a fish on. I trotted up to to see him reel in a Dolly Varden.

We had been fishing a half hour. I walked a short distance away and began casting again, and catching more char and rainbow trout. At one point, as Taylor stood by the boat rigging another rod, he called to me, "Hey cast your line down here." I obliged, and he reached out and dropped the indicator right next to his leg. It dipped under and I had yet another char on the line. It was that kind of day . . . plenty of big fish, but no pressure. Just reveling in abundance.

The next time Taylor called, he had more urgency in his voice. "Get down here, you're going to want a picture."

I saw he had the net out and my dad's rod was bent, line still running off his reel. He lifted and reeled, lifted and reeled. Soon the fish was in the net. It was my dad's first day of fly fishing, and he had a 23-inch rainbow.

"I'm not sure why you were worried about me not liking fly fishing," my dad said.

"Maybe because it's not usually like this."

We spent several hours like this, catching fish gorging on eggs. Then we piled back into the drift boat, picking up a few more fish as we floated downstream. We stopped to cast to a pool of silver salmon, but the fish seemed disinterested. We floated on, the water glowing blue in the afternoon sun.

The fishing slowed, until the pullout was in sight. Suddenly my indicator disappeared. I set the hook and the fish made a searing run. "Silver," said Taylor. "This is going to be interesting." As he battled to get the boat across swift current into the ramp, I tried to fight the fish. Taylor tried to keep me from dumping into the river. Finally, I pulled the fish up along the boat. It was not a silver at all, but a 23-inch Dolly, obese and colored up. Taylor slipped it into the net and then paddled a few feet to shore.

I've never liked fishing show victory celebrations; keep those hijinks on the basketball court. But I whooped and bumped fists with Taylor. It is times like this when you want to stop time, want the moment to linger. Want this to last forever. If only.

A few years ago, my wife and I joined our friends Scott and Nicki Hed at Rapids Camp Lodge in Alaska's Bristol Bay watershed. Scott is director of the Sportsman's Alliance for Alaska, one of the organizations on the front line in protecting this watershed. Scott had devoted the last decade working for Bristol Bay, crossing the country spreading the message about why this place was special. It didn't take long to see why.

Our first day at the lodge, we donned waders and motored up the Naknek River. Within five minutes we experienced fishing pandemonium. Not only was it a fish on every cast, but seemingly a different fish on every cast: a rotating mix of rainbows, Arctic char, grayling, jack chinook salmon, and sockeyes.

Perhaps what stands out more than the fishing, though, was our floatplane flight the next morning as we headed out on our daily fishing excursion. The plane lifted off and cruised over the Valley of Ten Thousand Smokes, part of Katmai National Park. Steam rose from volcanic activity, highlighting braids of rivers twisting through an endlessly green valley. It was, quite simply, the most beautiful place I'd ever seen.

To use the modern marketing parlance, the wild is Alaska's brand. The Last Frontier. Jack London Country. Into the Wild. A place of adventure and abundance. That brand may be true. It's also an Achilles' heel.

We forget that Alaska is not exceptional, not in a broader historical context. Once, the global norm would have offered Alaska's abundance. Thirty million bison on the Great Plains. Grizzly bears feasting on beached whales where Los Angeles now sprawls. Rivers everywhere churning with the runs of migratory fish.

Mark Twain once wrote a list of the quintessential American foods, the meals he missed while he traveled in Europe. As documented in Andrew Beahrs's interesting book, *Twain's Feast*, the author considered such foods as terrapin soup and roast canvasback to be signature dishes. They were readily available at any decent city restaurant. Try finding either on the menu today.

The abundance of Bristol Bay, and much of Alaska, is still here. But it won't be like this forever. A proposed project, commonly called Pebble Mine, would put one of the largest copper, gold, and molybdenum mines on Earth right in the Bristol Bay watershed. The Pebble Mine backers count on us to accept that Alaska will remain the way it is forever. That way we will see no great harm in putting this gigantic mine right in the midst of the world's greatest salmon fishery.

The backers of Pebble Mine ask the public to believe that *this time* everything will go as planned, that there will not be unforeseen technological failings—the kind that have occurred at nearly every other mine site on the planet. And this mine is not every other mine. It would include 10.8 billion tons of toxic tailings that would have to be held behind earthen dams. Earthen dams in a region prone to earthquakes.

The Pebble Mine proponents argue that their mine will not affect salmon, despite the fact it will be eight times larger than all of Alaska's existing mines combined. It would also require the construction of one of the largest power plants in Alaska to keep the mine running.

Pebble backers argue that they will be able to protect the watershed far into the future, even though the biggest project boosters acknowledge that the mine tailings will require maintenance for *perpetuity*. Forever. Does anyone really believe a mining company will stick around tending earthen dams long after the metals have been mined? Has this ever happened, anywhere?

They can make these seemingly outrageous claims because they're banking on people accepting Wild Alaska as a given. Can puny humans really destroy the largest salmon run on Earth? If we look at the state of other fisheries—fisheries once as productive as Bristol Bay—we can only regard this question as silly.

Fortunately, nothing has awakened anglers like stopping Pebble Mine. My friend Scott, who took us to Bristol Bay, enlisted the help of a long list of sporting organizations, individual hunters and anglers, equipment companies and outfitters. The sporting community can be fractured around environmental issues, but on this one nearly everyone recognized what was at stake. For his efforts, Scott was named *Fly Rod & Reel* magazine's Fly Fisherman of the Year. In the announcement of the award, Scott is quoted as saying he's "the worst fly fisherman to ever win the award." But his casting skills aren't the point: standing up for the fishery is one of the most important things any angler can do.

Since the mine was first proposed nearly fifteen years ago, the plot has been full of twists and turns. There were several times when it looked like surely Pebble would be defeated. It began to feel like Star Wars, though: the Empire is never really vanquished; often it's just in hiding. Waiting. When billions and billions of dollars are at stake, developers will wait.

One of the major victories in the fight came in 2014, when the Environmental Protection Agency (EPA) proposed restrictions under the Clean Water Act (a friend of fishing, once again) that would have essentially halted the project. In 2017, the EPA's new director, Scott Pruitt, met with Pebble Mine leaders and reversed course, undoing the proposal for restrictions. But then a big surprise came when he changed again, announcing that the proposal would stand, pending public comment. Some have argued that he did this because he fished at Bristol Bay, as did President Trump's sons. Whatever the case, from the start, this has been an issue led by anglers. They have heeded the call for comments. There's a recognition that this is one of the last, best places.

"Director Pruitt's decision was heartening news," says Chris Wood, president and CEO of Trout Unlimited. "But we have to keep our eyes on the ball with Bristol Bay. It's hard to overstate its importance to fisheries."

Wood says one of the most promising efforts is an Alaska state ballot initiative that would formalize protection for anadromous fish, making it more difficult to threaten or harm their habitats. "Historically, if we're honest, a lot of conservation has been forced on Alaska," says Wood. "This is an initiative that is Alaskan-made and Alaskan-led. Alaskans recognize what's at stake. The commercial fishing industry, guides and outfitters, outdoor retailers, and other residents have banded together to recognize the importance of salmon to their economy, culture, and way of life."

There's undeniably a sense that we can get it right this time. That we can still live in a world with salmon.

For how long, though? There's gold and copper in Bristol Bay. It won't go away. The demand won't diminish. A world ravenous for resources, and stockholders ravenous for profit, circle like vultures. Waiting.

For now, it's still here. Even in this crazy, crowded, growing world, there is still a place where you can catch wild, native fish on every cast. With your seventy-five-year-old dad. The best kind of freedom, the best kind of living.

We woke up for our final day of the Kenai trip and met Tim, who had agreed to take us out for a casual morning of rainbow and char fishing before we returned to Anchorage. We had caught more than our fair share of fish and this was icing on the cake. Tim, one of the older guys in a profession much less romantic than most imagine, was making one of his final outings of the season.

We motored from the lodge, up the Kenai, to the outlet of a natural lake. Periods of bright sun alternated with spritzing rain. We cast out egg patterns on ultralight spinning rods as loons dipped around the boat. And just like that, my rod bent, and my dad's rod bent. We started the day with a dolly double.

We caught fish after fish after fish. Fair-caught sockeye salmon, bright red and vigorous. Nice rainbow trout. And plenty of Dolly Varden char.

We fell into the routine: cast, let the egg bounce a couple of times, watch for rod jolt, set the hook, reel in the fish. We stayed beyond our planned time, stayed even after the fishing slowed.

"We're at forty-two fish," Tim said. "Let's see if we can hit fifty."

Lingering over us like storm clouds was that inescapable feeling that the trip was winding down. I looked around, taking it all in: My dad reeling in a fish, the loons diving by the boat, the mountains looming over that wild, flowing, abundant water. The fish. Always the fish.

You cannot stop time, of course. You cannot stay out here forever. Cannot stop the ever-grinding maw of development that seems hell-bent on reducing even places like this to something less than the sum of their parts.

But it's still here. Maybe that char on the end of the line is simply a reminder that for all our bells and whistles, we're still hunter-gatherers looking for prey. Or maybe it's because virtual reality will not compare with tripping over a salmon carcass while your dad lands his first fly-caught trout.

Whatever the case, as long as it's here and even a few people still love it, there's a fighting chance. A chance that we will not be fishing through the apocalypse, but just fishing.

Chapter Seventeen

Coal Creek

The woman behind the tackle store counter smiled. "You're going to have a great day if that's where you're headed," she said. "They catch all kinds of fish in there. You wouldn't believe what they catch."

She said this with a level of excitement that might suggest I was heading to the Madison River in Montana, or perhaps even Alaska.

I was not. I had just asked about Shamokin Creek, the water that flowed through my family's Central Pennsylvania property. Water that I never fished as a kid, because the entire creek was biologically dead. Water that had been dead for generations.

I looked around at the photos on the wall, some including this woman hoisting hefty fish. Shamokin Creek joined the Susquehanna River just a mile or so away. Surely she knew of what she spoke. I allowed myself a tiny bit of optimism.

"Where along the creek would you recommend I go?" I asked.

"What do you want to catch?" she asked.

"A fish. Any fish."

"Well, you can really go anywhere. A lot of people go up by the junkyard."

I knew this spot. It was not on Shamokin Creek. The woman apparently saw the look of confusion cross my face.

"Isn't that Shamokin Creek? Or is it Plum Creek? I always get these creeks confused," she said.

I tried very hard to hold on to my fleeting optimism.

"You should really talk to Sandy," she said. "He would know. He gets around by bike, and he fishes all these creeks. If you leave now, you should be able to catch up to him. He has long hair, and he's riding a bike."

I left the store and drove toward Shamokin Creek. I did not find Sandy. This quest was beginning to feel more futile by the day. I had long accepted that the "Coal Creek" of my youth was long dead and never coming back. I kept hearing, though, that maybe, slowly, things were changing. That maybe it was starting to come back.

I had come here chasing rumors of fish. I found plenty of rumors. I had not found any fish.

◆～◆

My parents grew up along Shamokin Creek in the tiny Northeast Pennsylvania borough of Snydertown. Their childhood homes were in view of each other; one of my mom's earliest memories is my dad walking up the hill with his dog, to breed to my mom's dog. My parents often recall a Norman Rockwell childhood existence, with neighbors socializing nightly on the streets, of church suppers and large gardens and the crack of baseball bats punctuating summer evenings. Much of the borough limits consisted of expansive woodlands, swamps, and fields, the perfect playground for kids to fish, hunt, shoot, sled, and cause harmless mayhem.

In many places, a large creek running right by town would have been one of the best attributes. Even in my parents' youth, Shamokin Creek was dead, running black from the coal being washed along its banks. Small-scale mining operations had only recently been abandoned in favor of the much larger mines in nearby Shamokin. Heaps of coal were omnipresent. People burned it in their homes. Many had family members who worked in the mines.

The town dump sat right along the creek's banks. Many people skipped the dump and just discarded their trash anywhere along the creek. One of my dad's favorite activities was picking up old bottles and other junk he'd find, tossing them into the creek and shooting them with his .22.

By the time my parents' relationship had evolved from childhood puppy breeding to the arrival of yours truly, Snydertown still offered a dose of bucolic charm—although it clearly was beginning to fade at the edges. The general store would soon close and some buildings had begun a spiraling descent into abuse and decay. It was still a fun place for a kid to play and explore. Shamokin Creek ran orange, and trash still littered its banks. It smelled of sulfur. You could see the remnants of old mines.

Shamokin Creek epitomized what ecologists call "shifting baseline syndrome"—we accepted this creek, as it was, for generations. A stinking, dirty, dead stream was normal, because that's all we ever knew. Imagining the stream surging with migrating shad and eels—as once it surely must have—was no easier than picturing mastodons stomping through the nearby forests. Mostly, I didn't think about the creek at all.

In the late 1990s, I wrote features on the environment and outdoor recreation for a local business journal. The editor assigned me a story about an effort to restore Shamokin Creek. I knew the town of Shamokin but didn't know the creek. I had always heard it called Coal Creek or Sulfur Creek. As I looked at a map, it dawned on me that this was the same creek that flowed through Snydertown. My family owned property along it. Since I was about twelve years old, I had touted my conservation credentials but had subconsciously written off the river that ran through my childhood.

As I researched the story, I learned more: that Shamokin Creek got its orange coloration from acid mine drainage, and that long-abandoned coal mines continued polluting long after the mining companies had moved on. The literal mountains of coal framing Shamokin once were forested hills with clear, little streams. Now each of those streams dumped a toxic load into Shamokin Creek. To turn things around, conservationists would need to install limestone filters or other structures to neutralize the acid. With so many acidic tributary streams, it appeared a daunting task. But the technology existed and was being used with success in other streams in Pennsylvania and West Virginia. Some people I interviewed thought I'd be seeing fish jumping in the stream in twenty years.

And now it's twenty years after those restoration efforts began. In present-day Snydertown, even the post office and church are gone. Some houses could generously be called dilapidated; others are just falling down. Maybe it's because of all the family history, all those memories, but I still find it pleasingly familiar. It's a place where you still bump into folks who talk about the crazy things your relatives did fifty years ago. On a recent visit back to go deer hunting, a man introduced himself to me by saying, "I am friends with your dad, I dated your aunt and I worked for your grandpa." The old-timers all still have multiple connections like this.

I still return to Pennsylvania every year, to see family and sometimes to go deer hunting. I came back this time, though, to see if Shamokin Creek had made any progress since restoration efforts began in earnest in the late 1990s. I came to do something I had never done in my life outdoors: to cast a line in Shamokin Creek.

———

Months before the trip I called Jaci Harner, watershed specialist for the Northumberland County Conservation District, for an update on Shamokin Creek restoration efforts.

"The creek has improved," she told me. "There are days when the water actually looks OK. There are other days when it looks really bad, running brown or orange. There are certain sections of the creek where fish have been documented."

Fish in Shamokin Creek? Could those 1990s dreams have become reality? In an instant, I began planning my next fishing trip. But before I could begin to get caught up in a fish revelry, Harner brought me back down to the coal-black earth.

"Unfortunately, we still have a lot of work to do," she said. "In fact, it is a huge, overwhelming task."

She explained that efforts were led by a volunteer group, the Shamokin Creek Restoration Alliance. The group successfully worked to install two passive treatment facilities. Passive treatment is essentially a series of holding ponds that remove a lot of the metals that cause the creek to acidify. While these methods have helped, active treatment—where facilities are installed to de-acidify the water and remove metals—is much more effective. And dozens of acid discharges still dump into the creek.

"In an ideal world, you would put an active treatment site at every discharge," Harner said. "We would prioritize which ones would be most useful to treat and work through them. But that takes a lot of money. The volunteer group puts a lot of time into this but raising the kind of money needed is just a huge task."

In 2011, the group conducted a feasibility study for active systems that would treat four major discharge sites. Just one of the active treatment facilities would cost $6.8 million, with an annual operating cost of $489,000.

"This is a group that struggles to raise thousands of dollars," Harner said.

Part of the reason raising money is so difficult is that local support is virtually nonexistent. A frequent theme in the Restoration Alliance's newsletter is that people accept the creek the way it is. Changing it seems an impossible task, and so no one bothers.

"Local buy-in does not really exist beyond the group," Harner said. "People don't care about the creek. It's sad to see the amount of trash there."

I asked what kept the group going. She said that every bit of interest helped. A local Boy Scout troop picking up trash might signal that younger people would care more. A call like mine could give a morale boost, just to remind local conservationists that people still cared.

I hung up feeling bleak about Shamokin Creek's future. Then again, she had mentioned fish. I texted my brother Mike, asking what he thought the chances were that I would catch a fish in our old haunts in Snydertown.

"I'll eat my hat if you catch a fish in Snydertown," he wrote back.

I booked my ticket anyway. Fishing, I've always thought, requires a bit of irrational hope and optimism. Many times you cast with only the dimmest of hopes that something might swim beneath the surface. Now it was time to test that faith in the most unlikely water of all.

My brother's pessimism notwithstanding, I began hearing lots of stories of fish in Shamokin Creek. A friend of my dad's had heard about someone who caught a trout, but it may have washed into Shamokin from a tributary stream (this, I would find out, was a recurring theme). One alleged expert on the creek responded to my email that he saw fish from every bridge. When I responded that I was on my way and would be fishing there, he quit replying.

There were even research reports that listed fish caught during biological surveys, although I couldn't find any that had occurred within the past fifteen years, and details remained incomplete. Strangely, many of these same reports noted the lack of aquatic vegetation and invertebrates, leading one to wonder what the fish ate. One study reported that the predominant life was bacterial colonies, with one hundred *E. coli* colonies surveyed in a small stretch of creek.

Why did I want to find a fish so bad there? Maybe it was like British fishing writer Charles Rangeley-Wilson's search for trout in urban London: "The world seems so knackered. I just think a wild trout in London would mean that it wasn't." I didn't need a trout—a carp would do just fine—but the sentiment was there. In our hot, crowded future, I wanted to know that fish could rise up out of anything we could throw at them. That even amid the coal-black rubble, someone might walk with a fishing rod, searching for silvery fins.

I clung to that image, that hope, for weeks. Then I got to the stream. I drove by it through the city of Sunbury, and noted that—miles downstream from Snydertown—it still looked orange, polluted. Nasty. I drove to Snydertown and parked by a bridge. As I looked down, the water looked like what happens when my toddler son mixed chocolate milk with orange juice. I just couldn't picture catching a fish in here. For a second, it seemed better that for most of my life I had never considered the possibility. The hope made the stream all the more depressing.

I parked in town, packed up my gear, and walked along the long-abandoned railroad track to the family property. My grandfather had tended cows along here, tasked with keeping them off the railroad tracks. One day, bored, he carved his initials into a tree. Those initials remained for more than seventy years, faintly visible as they expanded into a blob. That tree fell down ten years ago, but the area along the track remained thickly forested.

The area had changed considerably since my grandfather's boyhood. He remembered reading about the first deer in the area in the newspaper, and many residents disbelieved the report. Now, white-tailed deer abound, their signs everywhere. When my dad and I spotted a flock of turkeys here in the early 1980s, some neighbors asked if we perhaps had seen someone's escaped chickens. Today, large flocks of turkeys are omnipresent. On the morning I walked to Shamokin Creek with a fishing rod, I heard a turkey gobbling constantly. Black bears have returned, as have large coyotes with wolf blood.

On the flip side, an overabundant deer herd and warmer winters provide a perfect breeding ground for ticks. In all our outdoor play as kids, we never found one. Now, even backyard trips require thorough tick checks, as these little pests carry Lyme disease. Nearly every person in Central Pennsylvania has a Lyme disease story.

The hemlocks and ash trees have been hit hard by disease and non-native insects, soon going the way of the American chestnut that covered eastern forests until millions died from an invasive blight. The forest survived but has constantly changed with the seemingly endless pressures of humanity. It will not be wilderness again, but the wildness was still there, if you stopped to look.

But was the wildness underwater? It felt more like courage than hope that propelled my nightcrawler-laden hook into the murky depths. I'd periodically adjust my line. Nothing. Was I using the wrong bait? Did the recent rains make the water too high? Or was I fishing in water that had no fish?

Deep down, I knew the answer.

At a certain point, it felt like pretending—like those childhood games where your sofa became a boat and the living room floor a lake. You might reel in a shark, but you always knew it was make-believe.

I wanted to catch a fish. Casting my line was not enough.

I finally gave up and walked away from the family property, past a long, narrow farm pond that sat next to my grandparents' former house. It was one of the first places I fished as a kid, but I hadn't tried there in years. I stopped and asked the owner, Bob Buckles, if I could fish. He had worked for my grandfather, and said I could fish anytime. I got out my fly rod, tied on a small woolly bugger and cast out. Almost immediately my rod bent with a large bluegill.

Bob cruised over in his golf cart and watched, as I kept casting and my rod kept bending double as I caught bluegills, green sunfish, and black crappies. I switched to a blue cork popper, and cast to cruising bass, who smashed it with abandon.

I could have returned again and again, enjoying the aggressive hits alongside a heavy dose of nostalgia. But I wasn't ready to give up on Shamokin Creek just yet.

I awoke to the patter of rain the next morning, and looked out to a verdant, green, very moist world. I imagined the creek would be a roiling mess, so I decided to go to the city nearest the source of the creek and its namesake, Shamokin. It was once the quintessential coal town and now was, perhaps, the quintessential post-coal town.

In my youth, I remembered mainly the huge mountains of black coal that formed the backdrop to the town. Neatly kept row houses, many built by the coal companies, lined the hilly streets. No one would mistake it for fancy, but the town had a certain orderliness to it.

As I drove in, the first thing I noticed was that most of the coal mountains had reforested. Many even looked like natural Appalachian hills, with little or no evidence of their mining past. The town had not fared as well. Many told me that Shamokin had fallen on hard times, with poverty, high crime, and drug abuse. I drove down Main Street and immediately saw an immense man in pajamas blocking traffic, smoking a cigarette. Another car honked angrily as the man finally staggered away. I parked and walked to Shamokin Creek—at this point, early in its journey, only a bubbling brook. A small paved path ran above its banks. At a glance, one could almost imagine it as a charming mountain brook. But a closer examination revealed rocks stained a permanent rusty orange from acid mine drainage. I stared into the small stream but saw no sign of fish, or any aquatic life. Even its banks were largely devoid of vegetation.

I walked around the neighborhood. Those towering row houses with their large porches now stood in ruin. In my first ten minutes of walking, I saw five notices of utilities being cut off tacked to front doors. Other doors warned of dogs, or of people inside on oxygen. Some homes had been outright condemned. I couldn't escape the smell of stale cigarettes, mold, and rot.

I came around the bend to a large, ramshackle, three-story home, the paint peeling in wavy strips. Banners hung from the balcony, proclaiming "Make Shamokin Better Than Ever 'Together'" and "Wealth Through Coal." Behind the latter banner, a skinny man with a shaved head pounded violently on a punching bag. When he saw me, he headed across the street, aggressively said "Hi," then strutted away.

I wondered if he really believed that coal would save this town, save him. Would it suddenly rise from the ashes?

Or was it possible there was another future for Shamokin that laid in restoration?

My great-grandfather worked in the mines. I heard the stories growing up of how he went to work in the dark and left the mine in the dark. A frequently told story concerned the time his crew set dynamite to blow out a new section of mine. The dynamite didn't go off, so some of his crew went down to check out the problem. The dynamite blew up and they died. My great-grandfather survived the accident but later died of black lung disease.

He worked in those dark, miserable conditions so that one day his family would not have to—working himself up so that someday his great-grandson could do something like be a nature writer. I have benefited from coal as much as anyone.

But the coal industry, too, used up this town and its future. Jaci Harner told me that efforts to attract new industry to the region had largely failed despite low property costs and plentiful incentives. Industry executives looked at the orange stream and the falling-down houses and realized they'd never be able to get employees to move there.

Shamokin had gotten off easy compared to what happened to Centralia, a former community just 15 miles to the east. In 1962, firefighters set fire to the trash at the town dump, as they did every year. But embers from the fire ignited underground mines, setting off a much-larger underground fire with nearly unlimited fuel. Twenty years later, the problem became even more urgent when the fires opened craters in the earth. At one point, a twelve-year-old boy fell into one (he was rescued).

The town became unlivable. The government bought out landowners and eventually claimed all property via eminent domain, but some residents refused to leave. Today, seven residents remain out of a town that consisted of nearly two thousand people in 1950. Their row houses look strange and lonely on former town streets.

The last time I visited Centralia, my family stopped at the cemetery, where smoke drifted up around the gravesites. The trees had been charred off the surrounding hills. The whole scene was surreal, as if Cormac McCarthy's dark vision in *The Road* had become reality.

The mine fires stretch 8 miles underground. There is enough fuel for them to keep burning for 250 years. Coal makes wealth? Maybe. But it sure didn't save Centralia.

I continued my walk around Shamokin. A police officer talked to an agitated young woman, who kept repeating, "I never said I was going to kill him. That isn't who I am." I strolled past a realtor's office and saw a home could be had for $18,000. A woman complained to her friend that she needed a two-liter bottle of soda but only had a dollar left, and that wouldn't cover the tax. I couldn't shake the feeling of desperation.

I walked downtown, with many of the storefronts closed up. Then my eye caught a shop window with posters extolling the benefits of veganism. A banner on the door proclaimed it the home of "Coal Country Vegans." The light was on, but the door was locked. I knocked, and was greeted by an earnest, welcoming young woman.

"It must be lonely being a vegan here," I said, as I walked inside.

"Oh, some people don't get it but we're making progress," she said with a chippy enthusiasm. "The pizza shop down the street now offers vegan cheese. And I have every Coal Country vegan sign my poster."

She pointed to about twenty signatures, which did seem surprising. I tried to gauge what it was like to be a vegan in this town, but she exuded only optimism. She lived in what she described as an "off-the-grid, tiny house community" in the hills. "Our only rule is no meat or animal products of any kind," she said. "There are three tiny houses, plus a community center."

She had lived in Shamokin until she was thirteen, and then returned as an adult to start a vegan community.

"Why here?" I asked.

"I wanted a place to live in the woods," she said. "And I was reading all these magazines that were urging vegans to start their own community. They were suggesting Berkeley. Have you seen the home prices in Berkeley? Here, I can buy my own place. I can start something. Maybe others will move and this can be the vegan community. It may not work, but I have my place in the woods."

It struck me that in a world where there are almost no unexplored, uninhabited places left, perhaps the postindustrial wastelands will become the new frontier. The places where the dreamers, the outcasts, the renegades, and those with low-grade utopian visions will go to escape the conformist world. At one point, such folks headed West, to the wide-open spaces and endless vistas. Now they go to places like Shamokin.

Even Chernobyl, I knew, had been reclaimed by bears and wolves and herds of red deer. It was perhaps one of the wildest places left on Earth. The postapocalyptic landscapes have become the places off the map. Look just beyond the dreary town of Shamokin: the trees have retaken the hills, populated by deer and bear and turkey. And deep in those hollows, dreamers live in their tiny houses, building their own little worlds.

Life, indeed, will go on, even in the abused, forgotten places. But, I wondered: Will there be fish?

My mom wonders if my whole search is based on a case of mistaken identity. "Are you sure the people who see fish aren't referring to *Little* Shamokin Creek?"

A fair question. Little Shamokin Creek was one of the largest tributaries of Shamokin Creek. Unlike the main stem, people pointed to it as a model for stream restoration and community involvement. It was one of the most popular local trout fishing destinations. And while those trout were stocked, it at least could support fish.

On a warm May morning, I met Jaci Harner, the county's watershed specialist, as well as Ted Ramer, Scott Hixson, and Ted Carodiskey at the Long Center for Environmental Stewardship and Education. The three men were board members of the Little Shamokin Creek Watershed Association, and the center was their recently acquired property, purchased from a retired farmer.

As we sat under the newly constructed picnic pavilion, the men exuded pride in what they had accomplished and their plans for the future. They had installed a number of fish habitat improvements and streambank stabilization projects. There was a nursery for American chestnut trees, including blight-resistant strains. A pollinator garden was planned. They offered special fishing days for youth and for veterans.

Harner seemed in a much more upbeat mood than the last time I spoke with her. She said this effort showed what a few people could do if there was community support. "They saw there was an opportunity to get the community involved," she said. "And they have given their all to this project, from litter pickup to restoration to buying this property for the public to enjoy."

Carodiskey grew up exploring the creek, where he found eel weirs—rock traps to catch the migratory fish—from colonial times. "My wish list for this creek is taller than I am," he said. "But eels are a special passion of mine. Some believe that Shamokin, in Native American dialect, means 'place of the eels.' My dream is to see them return here."

We walked along the stream. It still suffered from siltation and warming waters from the summer. Stocked trout didn't reproduce, even if they survived the fishing season, but other fish species lived there year-round. Harner and the watershed group encouraged local landowners not to mow right up to stream banks and incorporate other conservation measures.

"My overall goal is for people to have a respect and value for water," says Harner. "I want them to understand the values watersheds provide, from drinking water to recreation to the ecosystem. I want people to know how the decisions they make about land use affect water, and how that in turn affects the community, now and in the future."

The stream trickled gently through the woods. It ran slightly murky from the rain, but compared to many waters in the area, it looked like a jewel. What if every watershed had such a dedicated group of individuals looking after it?

As we looked around, I mentioned my desire to catch a fish in the main stem of Shamokin Creek. Everyone had heard of the fish sightings. Everyone agreed that I should try closer to Sunbury, nearer the mouth where it emptied into the Susquehanna. They suggested a specific spot, near where Little Shamokin Creek joined the main stem. I drove there and found a series of posted signs. I tried to tell myself that these signs were all that stood between me and fish, but the orangish water below me suggested otherwise.

$$\sim$$

After I talked with the lady at the tackle shop, I decided to look over maps one more time. One thing I noticed about many of the suggestions I'd received and rumors I'd heard was that they were almost always near where another creek or tributary flowed into Shamokin Creek. I suspected that fish moved out of the tributary into the main stem of the creek. I wondered how long they survived there, or if they would be too stressed to feed.

But even if they were just recent transplants, it was something. In my youth, any fish would have gone belly up in minutes in the coal-choked, highly acidic waters. I just wanted a glimpse that a better future was possible.

I checked out several places where cleaner tributaries entered. All were marked by "No Trespassing" signs. Finally, I located an access point in Sunbury, three blocks from my high school. I went to a school where the first day of deer season was recognized as an official holiday. Hunting and fishing were far and away the most popular forms of recreation. But none of us ever went to this access point. I honestly didn't even know it existed. The dead stream ran through our school, too, but we just ignored it.

I parked and walked down to the water. My heart sank. Why did I keep expecting things to look better? It had rained more overnight, and the waters were even higher and murkier. I hooked a nightcrawler on a slip-sinker rig and cast, and waited. Nothing. I cast to another spot and waited. Nothing. Repeat. Repeat. Repeat.

I looked at my watch. I had spent all morning fishing the river thoroughly and had not seen a hint of fish. I packed up my gear and turned toward the car. Then I stopped. Would it hurt to look farther upriver? I walked, checking out the habitat. It all looked the same. Dirty, uninviting.

I saw a little divot up ahead. A tiny trickle flowed out of a treatment facility. A wastewater discharge. This was a tiny infusion of cleaner water—a 30-yard-long channel with water perhaps a half inch deep. Would that little bit of clear water and organic material be enough to provide a refuge for any fish that entered Shamokin Creek?

I cast out a fresh nightcrawler, and waited, with the same results I had experienced all week. I have a lot of fishing patience, but now I just felt bored. I left my line and walked up the little wastewater treatment channel, seeing if it held any life. Almost immediately, I saw little black dots swirling around: tadpoles. Thousands of tadpoles. A closer look revealed two half-dollar-sized painted turtles. None were in Shamokin Creek, but here on the margins they thrived. And maybe that was all that I could expect: the wild clinging to the edge of the apocalyptic. It didn't feel like enough.

I returned to my rod and reeled it in. The worm was gone. My hand rubbed the hook, as if to verify this fact. My mind raced through possible explanations: a bad cast, fast current, a snag. I ran through them again, but there it was: hope.

I stayed. I rebaited and cast again, and waited. Stillness. Quiet. Cast again.

At first I thought the shimmer of silver was an aluminum can floating downstream. Trash. I saw it again and recognized unmistakably a school of minnows. In the main creek.

"Holy shit," I said out loud. Then I sprinted back to the car for my microfishing gear. My earlier experiments in minnow catching were about to pay off. My heart pounded out of all proportion to the size of the fish. I pulled out my little Japanese wand, 8x tippet and size 32 hooks, and sprinted back to my fishing spot. I rigged up and attached a tiny nub of nightcrawler. I cast into the pool. The minnows had disappeared.

Another swirl. I lifted the rod and felt a tiny bump. I missed. My "pop" still needed work. I managed a modified fly cast to get the line back in place. This time I saw the whole school of fish swirl my bait, and I popped the hook. I lifted the rod, and had a silvery little fish.

I'd later identify it, using my field guide and social media, as a mimic shiner. It was a small, common, unremarkable fish, but I had caught a fish in Shamokin Creek. Maybe it was best to start small. I turned it loose, and then realized I still had a nightcrawler out.

The worm was, again, gone. I cast out again. I felt a bump. The waters were rising, and debris drifted down. Perhaps it was a stick bumping my line? I kept casting, and kept feeling bumps, but unconvincing ones.

My line sat still for ten minutes, and then: tap-tap-tap. Unmistakably a fish. I lifted the rod. Nothing. But that *was* a fish.

The light grew weird. I lifted my sunglasses, turned my eyes toward the sky. A bank of black clouds drifted into view. The kind of clouds you expect in *The Wizard of Oz*. The smart thing to do would be to leave, and quickly. *Screw that.* Those clouds would bring more rain, and then this creek would be completely blown out. This was my last chance of the trip. I cast again. Nothing.

I lifted up my rod and turned the reel, and my rod jerked. No subtlety here. I leaned back and set the hook, hard. My line peeled. I watched it go, in disbelief, then joy, then utter and complete panic. I fought the fish carefully as it ran upstream and down. I saw it, not a minnow but a real, honest, hard-fighting fish.

As it got closer to shore, I took a step, and slid down the muddy bank, right into the wastewater treatment ditch. I didn't care. I stood up again, and my legs flew out from under me, landing me flat on my back. Somehow I kept my rod aloft, the fish on. I glanced at my reel and saw it coated in mud. I stood up again, and this time plunged right into the Coal Creek itself, in all its glory. Later, I'd reflect that it was the first time I stood in those polluted waters.

And then, the fish tired. I reeled a few more turns, reached down and hoisted a fat, glorious smallmouth bass. A healthy fish, a fish that had been feeding. Maybe it swam up from the Susquehanna, and maybe it eked out its existence by this organic-laced outflow, but it was a fish. I released it back into the creek, wishing it well.

I wiped at the mud, and looked back at the sky. Conditions had deteriorated. Thunder cracked. The clouds roiled. My phone buzzed in my pocket: *Severe Thunderstorm and Tornado Warning. Seek Cover.* It buzzed again, my brother. *Bad weather here. Where are you?*

I gathered my gear and began my second sprint to the car. Trees whipped in the wind. My phone kept buzzing. I didn't have long before, from the looks of things, the storm would hit with full fury. But I had caught my bass. I had a fishing rod and plenty of places left to fish.

Lightning cracked across the sky as the first raindrops began pelting me. I instinctively flinched but kept on moving. It wouldn't be the end of the world.

Selected Bibliography

Behnke, Robert J. *About Trout: The Best of Robert Behnke from Trout Magazine.*
    Guilford, CT: Lyons Press. 2007.
Behnke, Robert J. *Trout and Salmon of North America.* Chanticleer Press edn.
    New York: Free Press. 2002.
Brown, Jen Corrinne. *Trout Culture: How Fly Fishing Forever Changed the Rocky
    Mountain West.* Vancouver: University of Washington Press. 2015.
Buffler, Rob, and Tom Dickson. *Fishing for Buffalo: A Guide to the Pursuit
    and Cuisine of Carp, Suckers, Eelpout, Gar, and Other Rough Fish.*
    Minneapolis: University of Minnesota Press. 2009.
French, Greg. *The Imperiled Cutthroat: Tracing the Fate of Yellowstone's Native
    Trout.* Ventura, CA: Patagonia Books. 2016.
Fritz, Richard, and Jim Rubingh. *Colorado's Greenback Cutthroat: A Fisherman's
    Guide.* Portland, OR: Frank Amato. 2009.
Halverson, Anders. *An Entirely Synthetic Fish: How Rainbow Trout Beguiled
    America and Overran the World.* New Haven, CT: Yale University Press. 2011.
Marris, Emma. Rambunctious Garden*: Saving Nature in a Post-Wild World.*
    New York: Bloomsbury. 2013.
McIntyre, Thomas. *The Way of the Hunter: The Art and Spirit of Modern Hunting.*
    New York: E.P. Dutton. 1988.
Plummer, D. Brian. *Tales of a Rat-Hunting Man.* New York: Lyons Press. 1997.
Rangeley-Wilson, Charles. *The Accidental Angler.* London: Random House. 2007.
Sartore, Joel. *The Photo Ark: One Man's Quest to Document the World's Animals.*
    Washington, DC: National Geographic. 2017.
Schmitt Kline, Kathleen, Ronald M. Bruch, and Frederick P. Binkowski.
    People of the Sturgeon: Wisconsin's Love Affair with an Ancient Fish.
    Madison: Wisconsin Historical Society Press. 2009.
Spitzer, Mark. *Beautifully Grotesque Fish of the American West.* Lincoln,
    NE: Bison Books. 2017.
Spitzer, Mark. *Return of the Gar.* Denton: University of North Texas Press. 2015.
Thompson, Douglas M. *The Quest for the Golden Trout: Environmental Loss and
    America's Iconic Fish.* Hanover, NH: University Press of New England. 2013.
Wade, Jeremy. *River Monsters: True Stories of the Ones that Didn't Get Away.*
    Boston, MA: Da Capo Press. 2011.

Waldman, John. *Running Silver: Restoring Atlantic Rivers and Their Great Fish Migrations*. Guilford, CT: Lyons Press. 2013.

Williams, Ted. *Something's Fishy: An Angler's Look at Our Distressed Gamefish and Their Waters—And How We Can Preserve Both*. New York: Skyhorse. 2007.

Wilson, Edward O. *Biophilia: The Human Bond with Other Species*. Cambridge, MA: Harvard University Press. 1984.